WOMAN ENOUGH

WOMAN ENOUGH

HOW *a boy became*
A WOMAN & CHANGED
the WORLD *of* SPORT

Kristen Worley *&* Johanna Schneller

RANDOM HOUSE CANADA

PUBLISHED BY RANDOM HOUSE CANADA

www.penguinrandomhouse.ca

Random House Canada and colophon are registered trademarks.

Library and Archives Canada Cataloguing in Publication

Worley, Kristen, author
Woman enough : how a boy became a woman and changed the world of sport / Kristen Worley and Johanna Schneller.

Issued in print and electronic formats.
ISBN 978-0-7352-7300-9
eBook ISBN 978-0-7352-7302-3

1. Worley, Kristen. 2. Women cyclists—Canada—Biography. 3. Transgender athletes—Canada—Biography. 4. Gender identity in sports. 5. Sports—Rules—Social aspects. I. Schneller, Johanna, author II. Title.

GV708.8.W67 2019   796.6092   C2018-904435-7
                                        C2018-904436-5

Book design by Five Seventeen
Cover image: © OK-Photography / iStock / Getty Images Plus
Interior image: (bicycle wheel) © boschettophotography / Getty Images

Printed and bound in the United States of America

10 9 8 7 6 5 4 3 2 1

Penguin
Random House
RANDOM HOUSE CANADA

For Graham Worley.

—KRISTEN WORLEY

« « « « « · » » » » »

For my family and for all loving families,
wherever we find them.

—JOHANNA SCHNELLER

CONTENTS

Gender Verification

《 《 《 《 《 • 》 》 》 》 》

"Do not show weakness," I kept telling myself. "Do not let them see you break down."

As a competitive cyclist, I had discipline. I knew a lot about riding through pain. But what these four men—all white, heterosexual and over fifty—were doing to me in this non-descript Ottawa boardroom, in the name of Canada's National Sport Organizations, was wrong.

Ever since I was a kid, when I would run as an escape from a life I didn't fit into, I had wanted to compete as a high-performance athlete. Sport is supposed to be straightforward, clear-cut. You train, you do your best, and you either win or you don't. Sport was my safe space.

I wanted to cycle for Canada in the 2008 Olympics in Beijing. I was ready. I'd spent the last few years training six to eight hours a day, seven days a week. I'd raced twice a week. I'd ridden through rain, sleet and snow, skidding on wet leaves and swerving away from countless cars. I'd made a million circles on the banked tracks of velodromes, climbing the steep angled corners and dropping down to straights at dizzying speeds. I'd gone to sleep each night with my pulse throbbing in my exhausted thighs, and I'd woken each morning almost too stiff to move, to do it all over again. Canada's national coach believed I would qualify fair and square for the B-team in pursuit track racing. All I needed was my licence. Which was why I was here, in this office, in front of these men.

I'm a woman, a fully transitioned XY female. But in 2003, in advance of the Athens Olympics in 2004, the International Olympic Committee (IOC), together with the World Anti-Doping Agency (WADA), had put out a two-page policy statement, the "Stockholm Consensus on Sex Reassignment in Sport," to govern the process by which transitioned athletes are "authenticated"—verified as the gender they say they are— and permitted to compete. It was now April 2005. I was the first athlete to be tested under this new policy, anywhere in the world.

Of the four men in the room, two were sport administrators, one was a lawyer, and the fourth was an emergency-room doctor—not a gender or endocrine specialist. The doctor had no special knowledge of hormone science. This shocked me.

I had assumed that the IOC would have done its research before moving ahead with its new policy. But an hour into the encounter, I was sure that I knew more about the science of my body than these four men and the entire IOC put together.

The assumed authority of sport had empowered them to do whatever they wanted to me. It was like handing a layperson a scalpel and saying, "Here, now you're a heart surgeon. Don't worry about the law; we answer to no one." It was absurd, and yet my sport and my livelihood—my life—depended on this panel's "verifying" that I was who I know I am. "Authenticating" me as a woman.

I'd already endured a humiliating physical examination with an endocrinologist in Toronto, where I live. He asked me intimate questions about my vagina. He did a complete gynecological exam. He requested and received an affidavit from the surgeon who performed my transition surgery, and a copy of my birth certificate verifying my gender as female. He asked me about my sexuality—even though who I like to sleep with is irrelevant to my gender description—and included that in his multi-page report. He shared my full medical records—*my most private information*—with this panel, who eventually shared them with the IOC and the Union Cycliste Internationale (UCI), the international cycling organization I belong to; they also passed my records on to Sport Canada and to Canada's anti-doping body, the Canadian Centre for Ethics in Sport (CCES), and literally anyone else who asked to read them.

I'm uncomfortable talking about sex. Even though I went through a full medical transition in 2004, I was a square kid, and I've lived a private, conservative life. So I requested a copy of the UCI medical report, and a list of everyone who had reviewed my private file. My requests were denied. "You just have to trust us, Kristen," was all the UCI said.

I was trying to play by their rules. I've always been a well-behaved person. Often too well-behaved. I am respectful. I treat others as I want to be treated. And I was the one who'd willingly driven the five hours from Toronto to Ottawa to be here, excited that, after this ordeal was over, I'd be able to compete in sport as who I really am.

I also knew that this was about something much bigger than just me. I wanted to make sport better and safer for the athletes coming up after me. I grew up in athletics. I'm passionate about the good things in the sport world, the way it's able to shine a spotlight on issues of ability and diversity. To empower people. So I answered their questions, even when, over and over, they asked me why I wanted to be in sport. I answered honestly: I've been a high-performance athlete my whole life. It's who I am. It's fun. It's my community, my tribe. My opponents are also my friends. It's about competing—for me, and for my country—but even more, it's about camaraderie.

To be honest, there was something deeper going on, too. I knew I was there to be *approved*. But what I really wanted was to be *accepted*. In my life, that's been rare, and it's precious to me.

I quickly realized, however, that these men weren't there to help me. They viewed me as a threat to sport. I was born in a male body, and their assumption was that an XY person will always, naturally and as a matter of course, out-compete an XX person. They had no scientific or empirical data to back up that belief. But their tone was clear: I was not, nor would I ever be, a "real" woman. At best, I was trying to cheat; at worst, I was a freak. They felt utterly entitled to ask me embarrassing, intimate questions about the details of my surgeries, and talk openly about my body in front of me, as if I weren't there. They had no idea that their line of questioning was socially constructed, as was their limited idea of "woman." To them, a woman—even an Olympic athlete—should be pretty and soft. She should look hot in her spandex outfit. She should be marketable.

I did what I always do when I'm under threat. I went still. On high alert. It felt like an out-of-body experience. I wanted to walk out. But I didn't want to show weakness. I was angry. I was on the verge of tears. I wanted to shout, "Do you ask male athletes about their penises? Their surgeries? Their medications?" But these men had all the power. They believed they had every right to do this to me, and they believed I deserved it.

Only once, when one of them asked if I'd have future surgeries, did I crack a little. "Yeah," I said to him. "I'm thinking of getting my ears clipped to make myself more aerodynamic." That silenced them for a minute.

Finally the grilling ended. I stood up. I shook their hands.

I drove home, alone. For five hours, I kept thinking, "What just happened to me?" They had my medical records, which explained my surgeries. They had the letter from my doctor, which clearly called me a woman. We were in Canada, where women and men are supposed to be equal, and diversity celebrated. They were the officials of sport, who claimed expertise about athletes' bodies. But instead of being open to learning, they were closed-minded. Instead of being professionally cordial, they were suspicious and hostile. Instead of being inclusive, they were prejudiced. They let me down in every way, and now they held my future in their hands.

I didn't allow myself to break down until I was home. Then, I cried for what happened in that boardroom. I cried for athletes all over the world who would have to endure similar humiliation. I cried for the bullied, misunderstood, lonely kid I had been. Bullied all over again now. Sport, my lifelong protector, had not protected me.

I didn't want to tell my family or friends about what happened. It was too private, too embarrassing. They'd already helped me through so much change, so much loss.

The panel's verdict was supposed to take three weeks. It took eight months. As I waited for the answer, as my most private information travelled in a five-page report from Ottawa to WADA to UCI, I finally realized what I was feeling: violated. Psychologically and physically, to my core.

My approval to compete finally arrived on January 16, 2006.

The letter, from UCI medical chairman Mario Zorzoli, essentially said, "Congratulations, you are who you say you are." But by then, something in me had changed. Of course I felt relief. I wanted to be back in my sport family. But I also knew that no one should go through what happened to me. Sport should not be sanctioned to humiliate people for their differences. No one should.

I stopped crying. I stopped feeling scared. It wasn't just about my competing anymore. It was about who isn't allowed to compete, and why.

I fought hard to be who I am—who I was always meant to be. So that's what I decided to do with these men: fight back. I decided to take on the Ontario Cycling Association, and Cycling Canada (CC), and the Union Cycliste Internationale, and the World Anti-Doping Agency. And then I would take on the IOC itself.

The men at the bottom of that pyramid, the ones on the local level, were the ones who'd violated me. But I was determined to prove how they were linked to the men at the top—how the 205 countries in the Olympic movement, and all their attendant sport organizations, and WADA, follow the orders of the IOC. I knew that the only way to make change is top-down. The IOC doesn't want the world to see its ignorance, or to learn that its policies are based on prejudice, not science. But I knew the science, and I decided to use it.

I didn't know that this fight would take a dozen years. I didn't know that my case would be heard by the Human

Rights Tribunal of Ontario (HRTO), which would help me to challenge both Canadian and international sport. I didn't know that I would kick open a door for women and diverse people around the world.

But I did.

CHAPTER ONE

The Platinum Triangle

《 《 《 《 《 • 》 》 》 》 》

It's hard for me to talk about Chris Jackson—that's who I was before I became Kristen Worley. It costs me something, some small piece of my well-being, every time I think about him. People want to imagine that transitioning—changing genders—is simple and linear and clear, as if Chris was a caterpillar and Kristen a butterfly. But it's not like that for me. It's like Chris died, and it's also like he never existed. I inhabited him, but he wasn't me. He was like a hologram, or a walking chalk outline.

It hurts the people in my life to hear me say this. Or maybe I should say, it hurts the few people in my life who were also in Chris's, because there aren't many. Transitioning kills a lot of relationships.

It hurts Alison Worley—Ali, my ex-wife—that I needed her to take down all of her photos of Chris and hide them away in a Rubbermaid tub in a storage unit. Yes, I had a wife. We were married for eighteen years—eleven years before I transitioned, and seven years afterward. Now she's a sister to me. I'll tell you about that, but that will be hard for me, too.

I'm not saying all transitioned people feel this way. I'm not saying I've entirely figured it out for myself. Gender is complicated; it's such a fundamental part of who we are that most of us wouldn't know how to begin to question it. I've been thinking about it my whole life, and there are still questions I haven't answered.

To understand Kristen, you have to understand Chris. I get that. But being Chris meant pain. Pain, anger, anxiety, depression, loneliness, discomfort, sorrow. So I hope you'll understand why I have to distance myself from him. He's Chris—he was me, but not me.

In March 1966, Margaret Theresa (Tess) Lynch ventured into the Spadina Road medical practice of David McKee, a Toronto GP who would later become the head of anesthesiology at St. Michael's Hospital. She was twenty-four years old, an unmarried Catholic from a village in New Zealand so small it was almost microscopic. She'd had a brief affair with a married man, Hugh Walters. Now she was three months pregnant. Hugh was thirty, Welsh, a chief engineer in the British merchant navy. He knew about the pregnancy. He wasn't going to help. Tess's sister Kathy and Kathy's husband, Terry—the only other people who knew—urged Tess to move away. She'd chosen Toronto because she thought her baby could have a good life there.

But now she was frightened, and she unburdened herself to McKee. How could she raise a child? She had no home, no money. McKee told Tess that he knew a couple who had one daughter, Jennifer, but were having trouble conceiving another child. He assured her it was a good home. He did not tell her, however, that the couple was his sister, Elizabeth McKee Jackson (who went by her middle name, Arlene), and her husband, James Edward Jackson, usually known as Jim. Tess phoned Kathy, who agreed the adoption was the best idea. The doctor's wife, Nancy, acted as liaison between Tess and the Jacksons.

Jim Jackson ran a lucrative business in architectural signage. His clients, including Cadillac Fairview, the City of Mississauga and the Toronto-Dominion Bank, owned the towers of downtown Toronto. Jim was dark-haired, handsome, athletic and controlling. An alpha male. A bad loser. An avid sailor, he was the 1971 World Champion in the Shark 24-foot keelboat class. His Shark, *Icarus*, which he moored at the Port Credit Yacht Club at the base of the Credit River, was more than his proudest possession—it was his obsession. (Interesting detail about the name: The boat was a well-known race winner before Jim acquired it, so he didn't want to change its name, even though Icarus is not the kind of mythological figure Jim would admire. He did, however, insist that the family pronounce it EYE-carus.)

Jim's wife, Arlene, was a University of Toronto–trained physiotherapist, who started the physiotherapy department at Orillia Hospital. She stopped working to raise Jennifer. Petite, bright, quiet, conservative, Arlene's default disposition was Pleasant. She ran the house, Jim earned the money. She never disagreed with him. Not in front of people, anyway. But at bridal showers, she would dispense a piece of advice: If you've been out shopping or otherwise amusing yourself, and your husband is pulling into the driveway at his customary 5 p.m. on the dot, quickly chop up an onion and heat it in a pan, to fool him that his dinner is underway. You don't want him getting angry. Oh, and have his rum and Coke poured.

Tess's child, a son, was born September 19, 1966. In the era's standard black-and-white baby photo, he looks calm but concerned, as if he already senses something is up. In careful script on the back, Tess wrote, "Born 19 Sept, 66. 8 lb 5.5 oz. At 1:45 p.m." Then she added the name she had in mind: Stephen. This photo would end up back in Dunedin, NZ, incorporated into Kathy's family album. When Kathy's children asked, "Who is this baby?" she would reply, "A friend of the family."

Tess stayed with Stephen for ten days. That's almost impossible to imagine now—a young mother spending so many sleepy hours with the son she's about to give up. She certainly would have bonded with him, and then ached over the loss of him. Though she never met the Jacksons, she wrote an emotional letter to them about her hopes for her son, which Nancy McKee delivered.

Arlene, an Anglican, believed in rules, in following protocol. She wasn't a soft or yielding person. But she did break two rules for Tess. First, she asked Nancy if Tess wanted the baby to be baptized Catholic. Tess relayed that Anglican was fine. Second, for three years after the baby was born, Arlene took out a personal ad in *The Globe and Mail*, Canada's national newspaper, on his birthday—unbeknownst to Jim, or to anyone. The ad began, "The baby born on this day is . . ." followed by a few details about her son's progress. Tess never saw the ads. Still, Arlene had tried to reach out to her, to let her know that her son was okay. Like throwing a message in a bottle into the sea.

On September 29, the baby, now called Chris—named for St. Christopher, the patron saint of travellers, because he had journeyed so far—went home with Arlene and Jim to a bungalow in Lorne Park, Mississauga, a few kilometres west of Toronto. A former apple orchard, Lorne Park is an upper-middle-class neighbourhood of tall old trees, playgrounds, schools, and well-kept single-family homes with lawns spread around them like wedding trains. The kind of place where kids walk to and from school each day in packs, and spend their afternoons riding bikes or playing tag until their mothers call them in for dinner. It was largely Anglican, conservative and white. (Chris can remember only one black family in his high school of 1,500 students.) Chris's new sister, Jennifer, was four years old. And as sometimes happens, not long after Chris arrived, Arlene conceived a son, Jonathan, born November 28, 1967.

Meanwhile, Tess was struggling with loneliness and depression. Through friends, David McKee helped her land a job at Canadian Harvester. But she would stare into every baby carriage she passed and wonder, "Is he mine? Is he?" Two years after Chris was born, Tess moved back to New Zealand and became a post office clerk in Greymouth. On January 29, 1972, she married Barrie Ernest Brown, a draughtsman, and they had two daughters, Katrina (born in June 1972) and Melanie (born in October 1975). But she told neither her children nor her husband about Chris until decades later.

The Jackson household seemed ripped from a 1960s *Ladies' Home Journal* article. Gender roles were clearly delineated—men were providers, women homemakers; parents knew best; and children behaved. "Hell" was a serious swear word. Jim wore suits to work—his office was attached to the manufacturing plant that made the signage he sold—and when he came home he always smelled like lacquer and paint thinner. He'd relax in the den with his rum and Coke, served by Arlene in one of the dozens of engraved glass mugs he'd won at sailing races. The basement rec room was lined with shelves of sailing awards, plus scrapbooks of newspaper articles about Jim's races. Arlene did all the cooking. Jim liked dinner to be prompt. His children weren't allowed to talk to him until the meal was on the kitchen table at 6 p.m. On Sundays they ate in the dining room, and, in summer, outside at the picnic table, with its orange and yellow flowered cloth.

The Jackson family had a rule at meals (and everywhere else): "We only talk about good things." Jennifer and Jonathan abided by the rule—they followed all the rules—but Chris somehow couldn't. From the time that he could talk, he liked to ask questions and express feelings. He could never accept that a pat reassurance or brisk dismissal were the only responses he'd receive. If he tried to say that he was hurt by or struggling with something, he'd get barely halfway into a sentence before Arlene would cut him off with an airy, "It'll all be better in the morning."

Early on, by the time he was three or four, Chris could feel how different he was from the rest of his family. He felt it literally, as an ache between his shoulders. Not just because he was blue-eyed and blond in a household of brown eyes and dark hair. From his earliest memories, he was never easy in his own home. He could never get inside what felt to him like an unspoken family agreement. In photos, he's usually on the edge of a group, or standing with another family.

When he was about four, Chris asked Arlene outright why he was so different from the other Jacksons. She made her answer sound like a fairy tale: "Your mother was Australian"— she was from New Zealand, but close enough—"your father was a sailor, a chief engineer in the merchant navy"—typical of her to know someone's rank—"and you are a chosen child." Even at that age, Chris somehow knew that this list of facts was the only answer he'd get. Arlene didn't want to address his feelings. She didn't want him to show that he had feelings. But the question—why am I not like other people?—was always in his head.

The Jacksons never hugged or held hands or snuggled up on the sofa to watch TV. Jim wanted his children to swim, ski and sail, but he didn't teach them himself; he paid people to do that. Raising children was a mother's job. Jim and Arlene didn't socialize much either, even though Lorne Park was a highly social place, where a convivial bunch of young parents were constantly getting together for picnics and cocktail parties, or going on holidays as a group. The women fed and disciplined and hugged each other's kids. They even had a name for it, the Mothers' Mafia. Jim and Arlene weren't part of it.

The Jacksons' bungalow, at the end of an up-sloping drive-way off Birchwood Drive, was divided into wings. In the children's wing, on the left, Chris shared a room with Jonathan. The furniture was utilitarian—bunk beds, a closet with folding doors, one set of drawers. The wallpaper was white, decorated with large illustrations of lions, giraffes, antelopes and zebras. The boys wore a uniform of sorts: white or blue shirts, navy-blue or gray corduroy pants, one pair of blue jeans. Though Jim made a good living, Arlene would buy the boys' pants two or three sizes too long, fold the legs under, and make eight-inch hems. Chris hated that. He was forever sticking his toes into the hems, ripping them; he was also embarrassed by the fade lines that would appear when the hems were let down.

Chris slept on the top bunk. At three, he suffered from an eye condition. His tear ducts didn't function properly, so every morning his eyes would be glued shut. He'd feel his way out of bed blind, slipping under the bed rail and reaching his feet for the ladder. He'd call out to Arlene, who'd unstick his eyes with a warm washcloth. When he was a little older, he had surgery to open his tear ducts. He couldn't help it, of course. But it felt like a weakness, a flaw that once again reinforced how different he was from his siblings.

Jennifer had the bigger room to herself: a mahogany sleigh bed, pale pink walls, a white shag rug. Dolls, Nancy Drew books, colourful outfits. Once, when Jennifer complained about having nothing to wear, Jim charged into her room, threw open her closet door, gestured to the clothes crowded on their hangars and yelled, "Look at this!" It was one of the few times Chris heard Jim reprimand her.

Chris looked up to Jennifer. For about a year, when he was four and she eight, she indulged him. When her friends would come over and play 45s and cassette tapes on her Radio Shack player (Chris loved its big thick buttons and how its cord twisted into a compartment underneath), Jennifer would invite Chris to hang out with them in her room. She and her friends would dress up and dance, singing into the built-in mic. Chris was enthralled. Pretty soon they were dressing up

Chris, too—as a girl. He loved it. Jennifer always shut the door when they were doing that.

That period didn't last long. Jennifer quickly became too popular to spend time with a kid brother, especially a kid brother who was a little, well, odd. Pretty, athletic, she was the girl everyone wanted to be. She was a lot like Jim—competitive, a winner, always aware of what others thought of her, and where she stood in the social pecking order. She worked hard to stay at the top. It would surprise no one when, in high school, she dated the captain of the football team. Jonathan was an affable kid, the type who goes along to get along. But he and Chris didn't spend much time together.

Chris began to be aware that he felt different at age four. It was also the age when Jim and Arlene began spanking him, frequently, for even slight infractions. Everything he did seemed to annoy them. He was an obedient kid; he didn't sass back or break rules. But any time he made a little too much noise, any time he was late, he paid for it. At first, Arlene did most of the spanking. She would take Chris into the garage or down to the basement laundry room. She'd pull down his pants and underpants, and smack his bare skin with a large wooden spoon, the very spoon that stirred the porridge Chris ate every morning in the winter. As she spanked him, she would tell him how her principal had caned her when she was in school—as if that made it okay to hit him.

As Chris got older, Jim started to take over the spankings, and that was scarier. He would grab Chris's shirt front, and practically fling him into the garage. Chris rarely understood what he'd done wrong—he just saw Jim's face darken, and he knew he was in trouble. Jim would warn him, "Don't you ever defy me. My father would punch me. He'd knock me out, and I'll do that to you." Again, as if Jim's history of being abused made it okay for him to abuse others. But hey, it was a family tradition, and the Jacksons loved tradition.

Lorne Park, Muskoka and the ski hills of Collingwood were the three points of a platinum triangle within which the Jacksons, everyone they knew, and everyone they wanted to know, existed. Inside the triangle the group-think went like this: Why would anyone ever leave our perfect, privileged paradise? What else could anyone want? Why would anyone want to settle for less—to be less?

The second point, Muskoka, was the fabled region north of Toronto of pure lakes, islands of Canadian Shield rock that glowed pink at sunset, and rambling family cottages. The Jacksons spent their summers at Bala Manor, a cottage and hotel compound on Lake Muskoka owned by Arlene's mother and father, Elizabeth Oliver McKee and Cecil Jon Galloway McKee, who had bought the hotel in 1946 for $20,000. The four-acre property had three hundred metres of lakefront. From the day school ended until the waning hours of Labour Day weekend, Arlene and her three kids were there, as were her sister-in-law Nancy McKee and her five kids,

Chris's cousins. David McKee and Jim drove up on weekends.

In its prime, Bala Manor accommodated seventy guests at a time, from May through Labour Day. Most were Americans on summer holiday. A seventeen-year-old named Gordon Lightfoot drove the Wagg's Laundry trucks for his father's family-owned business. Long before he was famous, Lightfoot would pick up and deliver the sheets and towels for all the local hotels, and would often sit in the lounge and play guitar for the guests. There was a full staff, but Elizabeth ran the kitchen. Chris and his family slept in a little cottage of their own, and ate in the main dining room, or on the lawn, with the guests. Adults sat at one table; the eight grandchildren sat at a picnic table lower down the slope.

After dinner, the waitresses would traipse off to concerts at Dunn's Pavilion (now called "The KEE to Bala"). They'd come back and rap on Chris and Jonathan's window, which was hinged from the bottom, and pass them paper bags full of string licorice. Everyone from Guy Lombardo and Duke Ellington through the Ramones, Blue Rodeo, Snoop Dogg and, later, Drake played Dunn's. Kim Mitchell was the headliner every Labour Day. When Chris was old enough, he went too; Jeff Healey blew him away.

Elizabeth was petite and brown-haired, strong-willed, hard-working and compassionate. She'd grown up in Sault Ste. Marie with four younger brothers. For a time she ran the Best Café in Windsor, Ontario, where she was famous for whacking a sailor who'd gotten out of line. She was Arlene's mother, that's for sure—they both could be controlling, and did not like awkwardness. But she also had separate, individual relationships with each of her grandchildren, and she was especially kind to Chris. As he grew older, she would tell him frankly that she could see he was starved for kindness. She was wary of Jim, but he had the financial means to contribute to Bala Manor's endless upkeep, so she put up with him. She had arthritis in both hands, saved every milk bag and scrap of tinfoil, and was always fully dressed by 7 a.m. The only time Chris ever saw her in nightclothes was the day before she died, in 1995.

Her husband, Cecil, believed in old-school gender roles. He was content to let Elizabeth run the place while he puttered in his workshop, maintained the physical property, and dozed in a chaise longue in the afternoon sun. He liked to get people's goats, and sometimes his teasing wasn't funny—he made racially insensitive remarks, and often said that women in his daughter Arlene's generation "had it easy" because they had washing machines. But Chris wouldn't be provoked—he'd see through Cecil's crotchety act and make him laugh.

Chris would rise at 6 a.m. to spend time with Elizabeth, who'd be up starting the baking—eight to ten pies a day, plus seven dozen cookies. Chris would peel apples into a light blue bowl while she rolled dough. With her, Chris would relax and let his guard down; he felt more at home with her than with his parents or siblings. When he exhibited a talent for drawing in grade four, copying Renaissance prints and wildlife illustrations, Elizabeth paid for him to take art classes at Hob Nobbery, a craft shop in Bala.

One afternoon when he was about six, Chris was sitting with Elizabeth in the glider on the deck. He asked her why he felt so different from everyone else. She didn't have an answer for him. She just hugged him (Arlene never did that), held his hand and told him family stories while the glider slipped back and forth. She understood the Jacksons' dynamic. She saw the way Jim looked at Chris, how often the man's puzzlement and disappointment gave way to anger. She gave Chris a reprieve from that, and that was enough.

Bala Manor was all about messing around in boats. Learning to sail and motor were rites of passage for everyone. When the children were small, they paddled canoes. Then Jim would take them out in *Snooper*, his antique sailboat with a mahogany strip hull and canvas sails. The mast was wood, the dagger board steel. Chris could barely pull it up with its nylon rope.

At eight, Chris and his cousins were allowed to roar around in an aluminum motorboat with a 7.5 horsepower Mercury engine, the kind with the pull-cord start. (The parents on the bay had gotten together and every family had bought the same kind of boat, to keep the kids equal.)

From July to mid-August, Chris and his siblings took sailing lessons three times a week at Kettle's sailing club, moving up through the levels from year to year and racing in a full complement of regattas, many on Lake of Bays. Because Jim wanted to race more locally, one summer he co-founded the

Bala Bay Sailing Club, and arranged for two truckloads of International Laser Class sailboats to arrive, for sale to local families. Lasers are small, one- or two-person boats, and Chris remembers their bright colours shining on the long, car-carrier trailers. The Jacksons bought two, and the McKees one. The sailing school provided boats—Albacores for younger kids, Lasers for older ones—but Jennifer liked racing in her own Laser. So she, Chris and Jonathan would clamber into their aluminum motorboat and thread through the channels to Kettle's, a three-kilometre ride, with Jennifer's Laser bobbing behind on its tow rope.

Chris liked the physics of sailing, figuring out at what angle to put the sail to catch the wind. He was successful enough to earn a spot one year in Albacores in the Canadian championships. But he didn't like competing. His best sails were alone in one of the Lasers, on days when the wind blew so hard that it drowned out all thoughts and narrowed his focus to simply staying afloat.

He did find one passion in Bala: waterskiing. He learned at age nine. By ten, he was already barefoot skiing. At twelve, he caught the eye of Steve Jarrett, a local windsurfer and skier. Jarrett invited Chris to be in one of the wildly popular Summer Ski shows run in Minett by Clevelands House, a sprawling resort between Lakes Rosseau and Joseph, and a popular local hub (its restaurant and bar were open to the public).

Nothing could have made Chris happier. The ski shows were the highlight of his summers. The skiers performed at least five nights a week. Every Tuesday they played Bala Bay, and a thousand people would come and watch. From the time Chris was six, his mother would let him go out Bala Manor's back gate and cross the street to the Prince Marina. Mrs. Prince let him sit on her dock, a thrilling spot, because the ski boats would roar in from the lake and circle the bay, and the skiers would swing out in arcs so wide Chris could almost touch them. Becoming one of them was a dream come true. That dream would shape his teenage and young adult years.

Collingwood, the third point in the platinum triangle, was also north of Toronto. A line of private ski clubs stretched along the highest line of the Niagara Escarpment, and Georgian Peaks was arguably the poshest of the clubs. Jim had bought the family ski chalet there for next to nothing when the club was being developed in the early 1950s. The chalet was a modest brown Pan-Abode with three bedrooms, a living room, a kitchen and a wrap-around porch, one of four houses in a small cul-de-sac off the main club road. The Jacksons always spent Christmas and New Year's there. Next door were the Wards; the two daughters, Mimi and Martha, were Jennifer's pals, and the father, David, was the Ward in Davies, Ward and Beck, a tax lawyer for the Reitman family. Across the road was Bill Rogers—everyone called him Buck—one of the club's founders; the club's centre hill, Roger's Run, is named for him.

Every Friday evening from November until the snow melted,

Jim would pull into their Lorne Park driveway after work—the kids knew their bags had better be packed—and they'd drive north on roads that often would be lined with snowbanks three to five metres high. Plows would roar past their car, spraying snow in an arc over the road. Chris knew they were almost there when they reached the flashing yellow light hanging at the intersection of routes 91 and 124 (though sometimes he couldn't see it for the snow). Chris was always quiet in the car. He didn't enjoy ski racing much, but that's what the club, and his family, expected him to do. It was almost his job.

A left turn off Hurontario Street—Collingwood's main drag, lined with red-brick-fronted stores and restaurants—and there they were, the ski clubs. Chris could rhyme them off in his sleep: Devil's Glen, Osler, Blue Mountain (the only public hill), Craigleith, Alpine and finally Georgian Peaks. The ski hills were on one side of the road; on the other, the waters of Georgian Bay stretched out like an ocean. The Peaks, as everyone called the Jacksons' club, had the highest elevation of the Ontario clubs, and was the only one that could host a World Cup race. Its Champlain chairlift is the longest in Ontario.

Hans Wieland, a skier from Austria, owned the ski shop where everyone bought their gear. That was a big deal: Wieland was a legend in international skiing, and one of the people who brought high-performance skiing to Canada. He was elegant and eloquent and when he entered a room, he immediately became the focus. He and his wife, Trudy, were always ready to help, teach, instruct and share their passion for downhill

skiing. Other neighbours included David Empringham—Emp—a fun-loving man who drove Formula 2000s for the hotshot Players team; and Russell H. Moran, the ski clothing entrepreneur whose DiTrani Ski Wear was one of the top lines in Canada at the time. His handsome son and five beautiful blonde daughters were the perfect advertisement for his gear.

Kids who didn't race—the so-called freestyle group—were outsiders at Georgian Peaks. The clubhouse walls were lined with black-and-white photos of club members who'd made national teams. A trophy case occupied the back wall; its shelves gleamed with silver cups with engraved labels: the Sibling Rivalry Trophy (Fastest Combined Times from Any Two Siblings); the Father-Daughter Trophy, the Grandparent-Grandchild Champions. Everyone got the message: this place was about winning, certainly, but also about privilege passed down through generations.

Starting at the age of seven, Chris was on the hill at eight-thirty every weekend morning, training for all three kinds of racing: downhill, slalom and giant slalom. He hated the hard leather ankle boots, the red wooden skis. The rope tow was always wet and icy; it would freeze his wool mitts and flay his sore, cold hands. He also hated his baggy, drab navy-blue ski suit, which matched his brother's. He longed to have fitted ski clothes in bright patterns like Jennifer's. (He was happier when skin suits—stretch unitards, acceptable as unisex wear—became popular for slalom races.) But he toughed it out, because he wanted to fit in. He quickly rose to the middle of the pack

and stayed there. High enough to be acceptable, low enough to avoid scrutiny.

In the evenings, when the west wind came in off the bay, the kids whose parents owned houses on the club property, including Chris, would have to lean in with all their might just to walk forward. But they'd gather outside the clubhouse, West Lodge, and bumper-hitch: there were eight kids, and they would split into groups of four on either side of the kilometre-long gravel road that ran along the foot of the mountain. When a car went by, they'd rush out and grab the rear bumper, and hang on, sliding in their snow boots, as the car towed them down the snow-packed road. On Saturday nights they'd go into the West Lodge and watch movies by the fireplace in the basement rec room while their parents chatted in the upstairs bar. The club had a chit system, so kids could sign for burgers and hot chocolates. There were banquets after races against other clubs, always capped by awards ceremonies.

Brian Stemmle, the national ski racer, was one of Chris's friends. The short, stocky Stemmle was fearless as a kid, always skiing too fast for his ability. He had a reputation for spectacular wipe-outs, but he had great air sense—he always knew where his body was on the jumps and moguls—and could fly eighteen metres. If he could stay on his feet, he'd win. But his family didn't own a chalet on club property, so he would disappear at four-thirty. Chris always noticed that. In the subtle things his parents said, he was made aware that being "one of us" mattered as much if not more than how one skied.

Chris and Jonathan shared a bunk bedroom in the chalet, too. One Saturday night when Chris was seven or eight, the boys were goofing around on the floor of their bedroom. Suddenly Arlene threw open the door and came straight at Chris, from behind. She began hitting him with the heel of her hand—on the back of his head, his shoulders, his backside. Jonathan burst into tears and asked her to stop—Chris remembers his tear-streaked face. Then Jim burst into the room, calling out to Arlene, "What the hell are you doing?" It was the only time Jim ever intervened on Chris's behalf.

Arlene ran from the room, grabbed her keys, got into the car and drove away. Chris woke up around 2:30 a.m. to the sounds of her coming home. Chris never figured out what happened. But he wondered if he and Arlene had more in common than he'd thought—if under her chipper surface, she was as unhappy as he was.

True to form, the next day at breakfast nobody mentioned it. That was the Jacksons' mantra, after all: "We don't bring bad things here. If you can't talk about good things, you're not welcome." Good things were defined as what had happened to Jim that day, or work. Bad things were anything unhappy, uncomfortable, personal. Chris understood that. He internalized it.

From the outside, Chris's life looked idyllic—rich with privilege and tradition. The perfect family, everything Tess had hoped for in bringing her son to Canada. So why did he feel so desperately alone?

CHAPTER TWO

The Switch

《 《 《 《 《 • 》 》 》 》 》

Chris hated keelboat sailing with Jim. Despised it. Yet every Saturday of his childhood, in the spring and fall, it was the same story: wake up at dawn, dress, pile in the car, drive to one of Jim's sailing races at the Royal Canadian Yacht Club in Toronto, or to Kingston or Niagara-on-the-Lake. Jim would already be there; he and his two crewmembers would have sailed or trailered the boat in. Arlene and the children would watch the race—though on Yacht Club days, Chris would sneak off to Centre Island to ride the carnival rides.

Afterward, Jim's crew would drive home with their families (and one or the other of them would take Arlene's car back). The Jacksons had to return the boat to the Port Credit Yacht Club, so Arlene would become Jim's first mate, while Jennifer,

Chris and Jonathan crammed themselves below decks for the long sail back. Jim would issue orders as Arlene struggled to manage the foredeck sheets and lines in the falling darkness. Chris would huddle, seasick and sick with anxiety, trapped in a stiff, cumbersome, red cotton-batting lifejacket. On longer trips, the cold waves of Lake Ontario, two to three metres high, pounded the deck, and the burnt smell of the Port Credit oil refineries bit the air and turned Chris's stomach. So did the sight of dead smelts floating in the green sludge where the Credit River met Lake Ontario. Desperately, Chris would scan the horizon for the Four Sisters, the lighted stacks of the Lakeview Generating Station, located between the Humber River and Port Credit, as a sign that they were nearing home.

During the week, the boat would sit on a cradle at the yacht club, and it was Chris's job (because he was small enough to fit under the cradle) to wash the steel and lead keel. Jim used Blue Slick paint to keep the algae off, and Chris would crouch for hours with a grinder, grinding off the old Blue Slick, which would coat his skin like blue chalk.

Jim, a perfectionist, was hard on everyone, but particularly Chris. He was quick to anger, a yeller. He'd trained the whole family to view him as the boss. He'd work long hours in his business, and then three or four evenings a week he'd be out practising, or preparing and moving the boat for weekend races. Saturdays and Sundays were occupied with racing. He left Arlene to cope with raising the three kids.

At age four, Chris started asking—begging—to be excused

from the sailing trips. Jim didn't like that; he wanted the family to tag along, to admire him. But Chris was developing a will of iron, and he persisted. Finally, when he was nine, he was occasionally granted permission to stay home. His sense of relief was indescribable—and not just because he hated sailing. Chris longed to be alone for another reason. It was his secret. It was a need.

From about age four, Chris felt like he had a switch inside him. Most days it was off. But when it would flip, he would feel it, physically. He was too young to know why—that his brain and his body were split, engaged in battle. All he knew was what he wanted—needed—to do. Chain the hallway door to the children's wing. Go into Jennifer's room, with its sleigh bed and pink walls and dolls. And finally, breathe.

At first, just being among her things—girls' things—was enough. He'd look at them, touch them. As he grew older he'd play with them, or try on her clothes. When Chris was six, the Jacksons got a white West Highland terrier, Corky, who quickly became his best friend and confidante. She was supposed to sleep in the laundry room, but Chris would sneak her out, lift her into his bunk, and talk to her until they both fell asleep. She also became his alarm. The rest of the family once came home while Chris was still wearing Jennifer's things. Mute with fear, he frantically pulled them off while Jim rattled the chain: "Why is this chain on? Get out here!" From then on, Chris kept Corky with him, because she'd bark when the car pulled into the driveway, and he could scoot back to his room.

Gradually, a pattern was established. Chris would feel the itch, the physical need. It wasn't something he could prevent. It was something his brain was urging him to do. The feeling came from his insides, and worked its way out. So he'd self-soothe, with Jennifer's clothes or toys. For a short while after, days or even a week, he'd feel better. But part of him also felt worse—dirty. Horrible. A failure. A freak. He couldn't even let himself think about it, much less think it through. And the idea of talking about it with anyone else? Impossible. It never even occurred to him. It would be like asking a giraffe what it felt like to be a zebra. Admitting that he felt such a need most definitely did not meet Jim's criteria for a good thing to say. No one in the family even talked about relationships, much less sexuality or gender. They talked about sports. Though Chris and Jonathan shared a room, they were never naked in front of one another. Only once, when Chris was twelve years old and he and Jim were walking Corky through Whiteoaks Park, did Jim awkwardly raise "the birds and the bees." Chris hurriedly told him not to worry about it; he was learning everything in gym class. But he wasn't. All Chris knew about his private need was that he wasn't supposed to have it.

In the summers, in the main house in Bala with its big bay window facing the lake, things were easier. Chris found a crawl space behind a wall and would stash clothes and dolls there—forbidden, girly things belonging to his sister and his female cousins. When the switch would flip, he would slip away from the lakeside and steal into the house, where no one could find him.

School was another challenge. From kindergarten through grade six Chris attended Whiteoaks Public School, about a one-kilometre walk from his house. He was small. He was picked last for teams. He was sensitive, easily traumatized. Simple things that happened to every kid—forgetting to do homework, getting hit in the face with a ball—would make him cry.

After a while, he learned to project a happy-go-lucky façade. He learned to pretend to be someone who fit in. He found a mixed group of friends—never the cool kids, but enough to get by. The path to school ran alongside his house, so a group would pick him up every morning. Chris would eat lunch at his friends' houses (though he almost never invited them to his). After school, they'd play hockey or soccer in the Lorne Park streets.

By the time he was nine, however, Chris began to find it a strain to maintain the façade. He kept it up, but he also started isolating himself. Kids would invite him to hang out; he began to refuse. They started to think of him as a loner. Not different or bad. It wasn't something that jumped out at them, where they wondered if something was wrong. It was just, "Chris likes to be alone. When he wants to hang out, he will. When he doesn't, that's Chris being Chris." In grade four, he was labelled a slow reader; he had to leave his regular English class to attend a special-needs one. That moment of scraping his chair back and exiting the room with all eyes on him never stopped being humiliating.

He didn't admit this to his friends, but school made his stomach hurt. The kids still came by to pick him up, but he got into a pattern of telling them to go ahead without him. He'd leave his house at the last possible minute and walk to school alone. His route took him across a soccer field and through a small forest that encircled the school. Bullies began waiting for him in those woods, six to ten at a time. They'd circle around him, call him names, sometimes hit him. To avoid them, Chris would leave his house later and later, and then run with his heart in his mouth as the sound of the bell echoed through the trees. His lateness routinely landed him in the principal's office, but the principal never asked Chris why he kept arriving after the last bell. He just issued punishments. The bullying continued at recess, and on Chris's way home.

Chris never told anyone. He was too frightened to explain it, and he knew what would happen anyway. Jim would sigh and imply that Chris was asking for it. ("What do you expect?") Arlene would throw him into the car and march him into the principal's office, where he'd have to name names. He didn't want to be a rat. And he feared retaliation. Jennifer figured out he was being bullied, and asked who was doing it. But Chris didn't tell her, either. He felt like he was living in a kind of hell.

As Chris got older, the switch inside flipped more and more often. It's not that he felt he was a girl. It was more like his brain was resisting what a "boy" was supposed to be. When his friends would marvel at some cool car driving through the neighbourhood, he would notice the hairstyle on the girl in the passenger seat. Then the switch would flip, and Chris would feel that he and everything around him was wrong. His clothes felt like a costume, a disguise, which he needed to change out of. He started swiping Jennifer's socks. They were colourful. They looked right on him. If he was careful enough, no one would see that he was wearing them, and if he had to, he could pretend he'd put them on by mistake.

When Chris was between four and six years old, the switch would flip once every few months. He'd wonder, "What just happened?" but then put it out of his mind. By the time he was seven, it had begun to flip every week or two. And when he hit puberty, it happened constantly, half a dozen times a day. He craved longer and longer periods with girls' things, and their calming effects wore off faster and faster.

A few times over those years, Chris approached Arlene. He'd start to tell her what was happening to him. He'd want to tell her. But he'd break down crying and walk away, and she never followed him or followed up on it. He had no way of putting words to the feeling. He was fearful of what she'd think of him, fearful of being a bad person, and so he kept on hiding his distress. He withdrew to his room for longer and longer periods. No one asked why. His family left him alone to suffer.

And then he saw the running shoes.

———

When Chris was in grade seven at Hillcrest Middle School, in the throes of puberty, he fell in love—with a pair of sneakers he saw at the mall. Nike long-distance cross-country shoes, yellow with a baby-blue swoosh. Black soles with a waffle tread. He put aside his allowance, five dollars a week, until he had saved up the sixty-five dollars he needed. He bought the shoes, he put them on, and he ran. At first, just around the fields near school. Then he began three- or five-kilometre runs after school. He realized that he not only had an aptitude for running, but it also made him feel free. As he pounded along in those shoes, he felt the world go away. The switch stopped flipping. His head was clear, his body light.

As a sailor, he was miserable. As a skier, he was nothing special. He had a talent for drawing, but in his family that meant nothing. Finally, he was good at something they could understand, even if they didn't admire it.

Jim's authoritarianism didn't matter when Chris was running. His mother's chilliness didn't either. Nothing did. As he ran on the park trails, or down along Lake Ontario, Chris felt a self-acceptance he'd never experienced before. Running quieted his anxiety. It stopped the switch from flipping.

Miraculously, it also helped him with his peers. After he set the school record for long-distance running, people began to accept him. The bullying tapered off, and then in grade nine it stopped.

He ran at Georgian Peaks, too. He'd ski until three-thirty, swap his boots for running shoes, and disappear. He'd do a twenty-kilometre run in well under two hours. Sometimes, for variety, he'd go cross-country skiing on the trails at the top of the mountain, which gave him another chance to be alone. Or he'd run up and down the mountains, off to the sides of the ski runs. The sight of him in snow boots, holding ski poles, dashing up the vertical heights of Roger's and down Champlain, soon became a familiar one at Georgian Peaks.

In Muskoka, there were fewer opportunities to run, but Chris's waterskiing accelerated. The summer he was fourteen, he picked up the phone and called Jim Bush, who ran the Supreme Water Ski School on Barrett Lake in Bala with his wife. Jim agreed to give him lessons. Chris would ride his bike to the school, three kilometres up Highway 169, and pay Jim whatever money he had. Jim taught him to slalom and to jump. That was a bit premature, since Chris hadn't finished growing. But he was good at it.

Really good. By the end of that summer, he was performing regularly in Clevelands House's Summer Ski waterski shows, though he was the youngest on his team by nearly ten years. He could do front and back flips. He helped form human pyramids. Or a boat would go out towing him and a few other skiers by ropes from the back. The boat would do a 180-degree turn and accelerate to 45 mph. The skiers would step out of their skis and barefoot back into the bay. The other guys were much bigger than Chris; the boat needed to really fly to pull them. He can still feel the sensation of his little feet bumping madly over the water, *bambambambambam*. But the crowds loved him, and he loved their applause.

His skiing wasn't about strength; he was never big enough for that. He had to rely on technique, more like the women waterskiers. But he loved the showmanship, the camaraderie, and his fellow skiers' skill. He especially loved the show's finale: a veteran skier named Bill Slyne would rise up in a Delta Wing hang glider, towed by a speed boat. He'd get to the top of the arc, three hundred metres up, and release his grip. The tow line would drop dramatically into the water, and Bill would soar straight toward the crowd like Superman, landing perfectly horizontal on the surface of the lake, chest down, on two foam skis attached to his arm pieces. It was fantastic.

That winter, some friends at Georgian Peaks, Heather and Dan Braniff, gave Chris a copy of *Spray*, a magazine for professional waterskiers. In it was an interview with Ron Scarpa, a seventeen-year-old sensation from Winterhaven, Florida, near the epicentre of waterskiing, Cypress Gardens.

The minute Chris finished the article, he picked up the phone. It had worked with Jim Bush; maybe it would work again. He asked the operator for the Winterhaven area code: 813. He called directory assistance, asked for Ron Scarpa's number, and dialed. Scarpa answered. Chris said, "I'm Chris Jackson from Canada. I'm a competitive waterskier, and I do ski shows. Can I come see you?" Scarpa said, "Come on your March break." It was that simple, because Chris was that determined.

After asking around, he found two university students who were heading to Florida in a straight twenty-four-hour drive in their Pinto. Jim and Arlene were used to Chris doing things on his own, but he was only fourteen; he knew he needed backup for this one. He called Elizabeth and Cecil, who were wintering in Sebring, Florida, forty-five minutes from Winterhaven. They agreed to keep an eye on him. The university boys dropped Chris in Sebring, and Elizabeth and Cecil drove him to Ron's.

The Scarpa house was on a court that backed onto a private lake, Lake Ned, surrounded by bulrushes. Every day of that March break, Chris and Ron skied together. In the middle of the week, another well-known skier, William Farrell—a US team member and world-record holder—showed up out of the blue, driving from his home in New Orleans in a blue Nova with his water skis on the roof. Chris was ecstatic: these were the guys who designed the coolest tricks. And they were teaching him.

A pattern was established. The next January, and every January until he graduated high school, Chris went back to Winterhaven, taking his course work with him. Ron not only recognized and encouraged Chris's talent, he became his water-ski coach, and the big brother Chris needed. Jim didn't want to pay for it, so Elizabeth did. In her seventies, she'd climb into her boat in Sebring and drive over to spend afternoons with Chris. She'd sit in the ski boat as he zoomed up alongside, and marvel at his progress.

In the following years, Chris would use the money he earned in the Summer Ski shows to enter waterski competitions: first in Muskoka, then across Ontario, then in Quebec and Alberta, and eventually internationally. The events were held on lakes, rivers, canals. Chris would squeeze himself into his tight blue ski suit—rubbery and thick with protective padding—and do as many tricks as he could in a fifteen- to twenty-second pass: 180-degree flips, toe turns. Each trick had a point value, assessed by the judges, who scored from boats or land. The summer he was fifteen, he competed in the open men's division, and came in second in the Easterns. By the time he entered grade ten, he was on the Canadian national waterski team.

The next summer, Chris stopped going home at night to Bala Manor, and (unofficially) moved into a ramshackle cabin with a bunch of other Summer Ski team members. In the evenings, he and the team travelled around Muskoka and across southern Ontario to do shows. (They also appeared in the annual waterski show at the Canadian National Exhibition.) By day, he taught waterskiing. That was where he first met Ali Worley: petite, blonde, pretty, she helped supervise the kids' day programs at Cleve's. They were friendly, but Ali kept her distance—Chris was a bit too much of a hotshot for her. Too many groupies. He shared rooms with various skiers (and often, their dates). He ate fish sticks out of the toaster, Kraft Dinner out of the pan. He earned a modest salary and—because the team was sponsored by the likes of Mercury Marine, Molson, Nestlé and Shell—some sweet perks. When Chris began driving, Shell paid for his gas, which allowed him to travel to as many competitions as he wanted. And Molson provided cases of beer, every self-doubting teenager's anodyne.

Strangers were giving him accolades. Full-page photos of him doing tricks were appearing in the Muskoka papers. But his family rarely showed up to his shows or competitions. Waterskiing wasn't a sport the Jacksons participated in or cared about, so his successes didn't matter to them. His siblings came to a couple of his shows in Bala. Once in a while he'd spy Arlene on the sidelines. She'd always come alone, and she'd disappear without talking to Chris. But the family never travelled to watch him compete; they certainly didn't go on any tours with him, as other families did. Jim never saw him compete at all.

Chris didn't care. He was happier away from the Jacksons. And he was getting plenty of attention. A-list kids with last names like Bassett (a long line of politicians, brewers, media barons and sports team owners), Rogers (more media barons) and Labatt (more brewers) suddenly began inviting him to outrageous parties, where boats were tied eight deep to the docks. Carling Bassett's island cottage, for example, had five boathouses. Arrayed all around them were the year's hottest new $50,000 boats, as well as priceless antiques, lovingly tended to. You'd tie your boat to the end and then hop into and out of each boat in line to get to the docks. The booze was top-shelf; so was the pot.

At Muskoka's Inn on the Bay, Tuesday and Wednesday were cheap beer nights, and the ski team would roar up in their 225 horsepower high-performance boats, which could hit 70 mph. Chris was drinking a lot, as well as smoking pot.

But so what? These intoxicants not only muted his switch-flipping, they allowed him to be "normal" in public, on the fringes of this glittering world. He was a shy teenager, without a real foundation. But as a ski star, he was welcome at every bacchanal on Lake Rosseau or Joe. Miraculously, he could still get up at dawn and train on two hours' sleep.

Then there were the girls. With his small stature, blue eyes and curly, sun-bleached hair, Chris was a perfect teenybopper idol—cute, fit, but not scary. Girls began phoning the ski school, asking where he'd be. They'd cuddle up to him in their bikinis, compete for his attention. They'd drag him into bedrooms. He'd deflect. Chris's friends were dating girls, but he had no desire to, and he didn't understand why. He tried to fantasize about girls, but couldn't. He wasn't even masturbating—he suppressed any feelings he had in that area. He knew he wasn't gay. He'd had that discussion with himself when he first hit puberty, and his switch started flipping like crazy. Whatever the switch was about, he was sure it wasn't men. So he played along when girls came on to him, just enough to appear to fit in.

Chris had discovered that he could wear this New Chris, Waterskier Chris, like a suit of armour. Real Chris had real problems. But this shaggy-haired, super-skier party guy? People liked him. The persona offered him some protection.

Thanks to New Chris, high school became a little easier. A little. Lorne Park Secondary School was straight out of a John

Hughes movie: there were hierarchies, and football was at the top. The jocks and cheerleaders were the pinnacle of the social pyramid; their teachers looked to them as the school leaders. Thanks to an affiliation with Ohio State University, LPSS even had fraternities and sororities.

Chris began hanging out with the school's other high-performance athletes, including the rower Silken Laumann, who was three years older. The kids got used to hearing his name announced over the PA system, after he'd won a cross-country meet. At home, he spent most of his time in the basement rec room with Corky. He was taking greater and greater chances, putting on women's clothes even when his parents were upstairs. But he made sure no one knew that.

When he was sixteen, the James Bond movie *For Your Eyes Only* came out. A gorgeous extra in the film, Tula, was a model in the UK. A few months later, tabloids ran the headline, "Bond Girl Is a Boy." Tula (Caroline Cossey) had been born with a genetic variation: instead of XX, she was XXY. She lived the first part of her life as a male, and then transitioned to female. How strange, Chris thought. How scary. How . . . fascinating. He was as interested in the idea as he was afraid of it. "This can't be what I have," he thought. "That would make me really weird." Yet, when the switch flipped and he snuck into Jennifer's room, he felt a sense of rightness—for a few minutes, until the feeling that he was dirty washed over him. But was he like Tula? Could he do what she had done? "I can't," he thought. "That can't be it."

To quiet those fears, he stepped up his running, his cross-training. He often worked out with Laumann and Jane Vincent, a cross-country skier. Chris liked hanging out with girls more than boys—conversation was easier, and he could be more himself, without the pressure to present as ultra-male.

Then Chris invested some of his waterski money in a racing bike, a black Nishiki with gold trim. Riding gave him the same sense of freedom that running did, and more independence. As a serious cyclist, he could also shave his legs, which he liked; it was even more calming to his switch than wearing Jennifer's socks. He'd hop on his bike, and in a few minutes he'd be in North Oakville, which was still farmland.

Soon he was running five kilometres every morning, and biking every afternoon. The school bell went at 3 p.m.; by 3:15 he'd be on his bike. He'd bike for three hours, 75 to 120 kilometres. Then he'd go for an evening run, thirteen kilometres through the ravines.

On a cold day in October when he was seventeen, Chris ran his first Toronto marathon. He hadn't trained. He didn't even know how the starting line worked. But he was so fit from running and cycling, he ran it in 2 hours 58 minutes (which put him in the top 30 percent of runners his age).

After the race, Chris was standing, wrapped in a foil blanket, in a huge crowd outside the old Varsity Stadium on Bloor Street West. A man approached him—Mr. Olcina, a Czech immigrant who'd been a carpenter in Jim's company. He was a puppeteer, and used to entertain kids with puppet shows. He'd once given Chris a puppet, a polar bear named Uchi, which means "black eyes." Chris hadn't seen him since he was a kid, but Olcina had recognized him among the runners. "I had to come and see you!" Olcina said, smiling. He gave Chris a big hug, and disappeared. Chris remembers that so clearly. He remembers most of the times someone touched him as he was growing up, because his family so rarely did.

Chris hoped that Jim would approve of his athletic successes. But Jim wanted Chris to play football. LPSS had a string of championship-winning teams, and Jonathan played football. When Chris was in grade eleven, Jim insisted he try out.

Imagine the scene: Late-summer training camp. Monster-sized guys on the field, most of whom had been playing since grade school. Out comes this slight figure, five feet six, 116 pounds, holding a helmet under his arm. He doesn't know the drills. He needs to safeguard his knees for waterskiing. He doesn't know how to tackle, or how to protect himself while being tackled.

It was a slaughter. The coaches weren't sympathetic: "Toughen up and get back in, or get off the field." Chris's friend K.C., a lifelong football player, was across the field doing drills. "What is Chris doing here?" he wondered. "This is not a game you just walk into." After practice K.C. stayed behind and showed Chris a few moves, some techniques to fend off tacklers. But it was too late. On the second day of tryouts, Gary Johnson, the school's best linebacker at six foot one and 170 pounds, picked Chris up and threw him down. Chris walked off the field and never went back.

Jim didn't say much about it, but Chris knew he was disappointed. Jim respected certain qualities, and if you didn't have them, you weren't ever going to measure up in his eyes. Chris had many of those qualities—motivation, discipline, commitment. But he was missing a crucial one: he didn't have the killer instinct.

As Chris got older, Jim's anger toward him erupted more often, with less provocation. One afternoon at a private club in Muskoka, Jim challenged Chris to a game of tennis. Jim played highly competitive tennis several times a week. Chris played occasionally; mostly he'd just bat the ball around. But on this day Chris started winning. Jim began returning the ball harder and harder over the net. Then he began aiming it at Chris. Mid-game, Chris put his racket down, said, "This isn't fun anymore," and walked off. As always, they never spoke about it.

On any given day, Chris would be going about his business. Suddenly he'd become aware that Jim was staring at him. Jim's face would twist with disgust. His pupils would dilate, turning his eyes black. The next thing Chris knew, Jim would be on him, throwing punches. One evening at Bala Manor, Chris was merely walking across the front lawn when Jim flew at him out of nowhere. Elizabeth witnessed it through the kitchen window. Later, when they were alone, she told Chris, "I don't know why he does that to you and not to your siblings." That might not have been strictly true. She might have known why, but either didn't have the words for it, or didn't want to say them. But she let Chris know that she saw him and felt for him, and to him that was a lot.

To quiet his switch, Chris was over-training. But that created another problem. He wasn't skipping only dinner to go running. He was skipping most meals. He was down to less than 6 percent body fat.

He needed fuel for his training though, so his solution was to drink three litres of milk a day. The occasions when his family forced him to sit down to dinner, he'd push his food around and drink a litre-bag of milk instead. In a corner of his mind, a word appeared: anorexia. But he pushed the thought away. Boys weren't anorexic! Not eating was just a way of asserting control over his uncontrollable switch. If it was also a reaction against his physical development as a male—well, he didn't want to think about that either. Whatever it was inside him that was calling him to be different, he couldn't face it. He developed a tic: at his desk in class, or on his sofa at home, he'd repeatedly smack his thigh with the back of his hand, swatting whatever It was away.

His parents were concerned enough by his weight loss that they sent him to the Fitness Institute in Mississauga, where he saw a sport specialist and a nutritionist. Gradually, the nutritionist got Chris eating again, but he never weighed more than 125 pounds. Jim added shame to this equation: often he would say to Jonathan and Jennifer, "We can't go to Collingwood again this weekend because Chris has to go to the doctor."

Not surprisingly, Chris's grades began to slip. In addition to his special-ed reading class, he was assigned to special-ed math. Luckily, the teacher, Mr. Ash, became an ally. The hallways of LPSS were lined with photos of famed football players, but after Chris went to the world championships in waterskiing, Mr. Ash put a photo of Chris on skis in his office. That helped. So did Chris's cross-country coach, Ms. Ann Scott, who sensed his difference and gave him space and compassion. His art teacher, Ms. Stinner, was also supportive; the art room was Chris's refuge. He spent a lot of time there making pastel and charcoal illustrations.

By grade eleven, high school socializing became difficult even for New Chris. The Lorne Park kids, who could be found smoking and drinking at someone's house most weekends, would invite him. More and more often, he'd say no. He never said to his friend K.C., or any of them, "I don't feel comfortable." He said, "It's Friday night, I have to train, I'm going for a forty K on my bike." Eventually, his friends began to feel that they were badgering him, and they stopped asking. It wasn't malicious. They weren't cutting him out—he was doing that to himself. The kids who used to pick him up on their way to school still used the path by his house that led to the football field. But now they walked by and didn't stop.

Eventually he did most of his hanging out with one friend, Guido Hafer. Guido straddled a few social groups. He was mechanically minded, a bit geeky. He liked fixing bikes and other machinery. Guido's dad sold waffle makers, and he'd pay Guido and Chris ten dollars apiece for assembling them. Chris knew that Guido's father was authoritative and over-bearing, like Jim. They didn't talk much about it. But they found a refuge in one another.

Guido and Chris did a lot of cycling together, often joined by Michelle, another friend. The three also spent long hours hanging out in Guido's basement, listening to Yes and Led Zeppelin. Sometimes when they were straddling their bikes, taking a break from riding, they'd be talking and laughing, and suddenly Chris would just zone out. He'd stand with his head down, his eyes down. He was there, but gone. After a minute or two, Michelle would wave a hand in front of Chris's face, say "Hey!" and elbow him—and he'd come back. They didn't know that was his switch flipping, that the pressure of pretending had built up, and he needed to disconnect from his life for a few beats. They just accepted it as part of him.

Guido convinced Chris to go to the occasional party. But when Chris would start drinking, he wouldn't stop. He wasn't a happy drunk. He'd get loaded and disappear. K.C. or some-one would find him outside sitting in a tree, railing at himself: "Why am I here, why am I not training? I shouldn't be drunk. This is going to set me back." His anger was palpable. If some-one said, "Don't worry, it's only one night," Chris would shout back, "NO! It's not!"

Chris was fighting for self-control. To do that, he had to con-trol his relationships with people, and the amount of engagement he had with them. When the anxiety became too much, he isolated himself, a pattern that continued into adulthood. But it wasn't making him happy. In fact, he was getting worse.

One July day when he was seventeen, on a visit to Bala Manor, Chris felt overwhelmed. All his efforts at control—the training, the drinking, the skiing—were failing. He was depressed, anxious, under-slept. Exhausted. Imploding. He had no one he could turn to. "I can't do this anymore," he thought.

He walked down to the little cove between the boathouse and the main dock. The family called it "Grandma's Cove," because Elizabeth used to swim off the point. It was her place to go to take a break. Chris felt close to her here. It might be hard to understand, but it's why he chose this place to do what he did next. He waded into the water, then dived under. He thought if he could wedge himself into the large rocks that filled the cribbing under the boathouse, he could stay under. Forever.

He didn't think that killing himself would be a selfish act. If anything, he thought his family would feel relieved. He was always the problem child, the mistake, the kid Jim and Arlene brought into their family who'd been nothing but trouble since. He felt like the Jacksons and their cohort clicked together like a picture puzzle, but he was the wrong size and shape. As hard as they tried, and as hard as he tried, he couldn't be made to fit. "I want to be part of this," he thought, "but I can't."

Under the surface, Chris felt calm. The water was warm and clear, maybe two-and-a-half metres deep. He loved the sound it made splashing under the dock. When his body would bob up, he would take another breath and force it back under. It went on for a long time, perhaps forty-five minutes. He came close to unconsciousness once or twice. But eventually he gave up. Something was stopping him.

Walking back to the house, he felt tired, shut down. Shut off. The desperation was gone. He didn't feel relief, but that particular moment had passed.

He glanced back—two dozen of his family members were lying on the beach and playing in the water about 150 metres from where he'd tried to end his life. They had no idea. At 7 p.m., they gathered for dinner as usual. Chris joined them.

That's the thing about the walls you build around yourself. You think they'll protect you. By the time you realize they don't, it's too late. You built them too high, too sturdily; they're impossible to tear down. How could you tell everyone in your life that you're not who they think you are? You can't. So you become a person nobody really knows.

CHAPTER THREE

So This Is Love

« « « « « • » » » » »

By the time Chris graduated from grade thirteen, with the help of correspondence courses, he'd been a ranking water-skier for three years. He'd been to the Water Ski World Championships, and had never placed below sixth in a competition. Because he was also cross-training more rigorously on the bicycle, his body was changing shape—from the physique of a waterskier, whose bulk is in the shoulders, to that of a cyclist, who is strongest in the thighs.

An idea began to itch at Chris. He wanted to go to the Olympics. It's the splashiest sporting event in the world, the pinnacle of amateur athletics. If Chris could make it to the Olympics, would his family finally accept him? Would he accept himself?

He already had the discipline. He was easy to coach. He knew how to compete. Waterskiing wasn't an Olympic sport, but cycling was. Cycling, he decided, was his way in.

Chris visited a cycle shop in Mississauga to upgrade to a high-performance bike. The owner of the shop, Rob Jones, was a retired road racer who was also the editor of *Canadian Cycling* magazine. He invited Chris to join his cycling club.

Within a year, Chris was riding at the elite level, taking part in national championship rides with the store's team, often placing second or third. He got sponsors for his shoes, for his pedals. He was training nearly full-time. In winter, he and Jones rented a house in South Carolina and rode all day every day, 140 to 160 kilometres in two back-to-back rides. Sleep, eat, cycle—that was his life. His teammates, who were older and larger, called him TBT, Tiny But Tough. He could handle mountain drills, speed drills. He could take his turn at the front of the peloton, letting the others draft him. He could cope with the sore backside, the screaming quads and calves, and the intestinal havoc that riding wreaked. It also helped with his switch—waterskiing has a short season, but cycling offered a daily escape.

His third year with the team was the best season of his life. The Olympics felt like they were right in front of him. In a national competition, a 110-kilometre road race in St. Catharines, Ontario, on a summer Sunday in 1988, Chris was in tenth place at the final kilometre mark. He was facing a long downhill, followed by a short uphill sprint to the finish.

It was hot, in the mid-30s Celsius. The wind was at his back. As always happens in the last kilometre of a long race, the seventy-five-odd riders began jostling for their final position. Anticipating where he wanted to be for the uphill sprint, Chris spotted a window on his left. Smoothly, carefully, he transferred left on the downhill. Suddenly, the rider in third position shot sideways across the pack, without checking where the other riders around him were. At 60 km/h. He caught two riders beside Chris, then Chris. After that, all Chris can remember clearly is the sound of screeching brakes.

He went up over his front wheel, rotated to his right, and hit the ground hard. He was locked into his bike, so he took the whole hit with his hip. Luckily, he didn't slide on the asphalt, which would have ripped open his skin.

It was one of the worst crashes in Canadian cycling. In all, two dozen riders went down. Bikes costing $8,000 apiece were destroyed. All around Chris, riders broke shoulders, suffered concussions. In shock, Chris stood up and hobbled a few steps. His last thought was, "This kills, this kills." Then he crumpled to the ground, unconscious.

He remembers someone strapping him onto a backboard. He didn't know why he was in shock until the EMTs tightened the strap around his hip. Then he knew. He screamed in pain. His hipbone was broken, a four-inch crack in his ilium.

After only twenty-four hours, the hospital sent him home to Lorne Park with a bunch of painkillers. It would be six months before he could walk again, and a year before he got on a racing bike. This was bad news for his mental health. Riding a bike had become a necessity, an addiction, for Chris. It's why he could ride six or eight hours a day. Merely climbing onto the seat gave him an endorphin rush. Trapped at home after the accident, with people who didn't exactly love him, Chris needed to get back to that feel-good place.

The minute he could lift his leg high enough, he went into the garage and dug out his mother's Raleigh three-speed. A girl's bike, it had a down tube instead of a cross bar, and a big seat with generous suspension. Though he wasn't supposed to, he eased a leg over the tube and straddled the seat, to see if he could stand it. He did it every day. He knew he couldn't possible sit on a hard, lean racing saddle. But he had to get on a bike, any bike, even for a few seconds. No matter how much it hurt, it hurt more not to.

Something else was changing in Chris's life—something huge. For the first time, he was falling in love. A few months before his accident, in the spring of 1988, he had visited some Lorne Park classmates at Trent University, an impressive group of concrete buildings designed by the architect Ron Thom, arrayed along the Otonabee River in Peterborough, Ontario. The campus was crowded—it was the weekend of the annual Head of the Trent, a multi-university rowing competition. Chris and his friends were in the Pig's Ear, a typical student pub—wooden floors, long picnic-style tables, draft beer in little cups that you'd buy in trays of twenty, ridiculously cheap because it was carbonated. It caused the worst hangovers, but no one cared because, well, it was ridiculously cheap. The bar was famous for its peanut races: players dropped a salted peanut into their beer cups; the peanut would sink, then start to rise; the player with the last peanut up had to drain his or her cup in one go.

In the middle of a peanut race, Chris spotted Ali Worley in a far corner. He hadn't seen her in years, since they worked together at Clevelands House on Lake Rosseau. Now she was an English major at Trent. Suddenly, like a scene in a movie, the long tables of chattering friends, the noisy peanut races, fell away. There were conversations all around them, but Chris and Ali were having *the* conversation.

Can you imagine how relieved he felt? A normal response to a woman. A normal relationship. In the summer, when Ali moved back to her family's home in the Beach—a funky Toronto neighbourhood by Lake Ontario, with a strip of shops and restaurants on Queen Street East, and a long boardwalk that ran over miles of sandy lakeshore—Chris wooed her hard. With his waterskiing money, he bought a car; he'd pick her up and take her to fancy restaurants three nights a week. He must have spent $10,000 that summer, but he didn't care. She was everything he could want: lovely, smart, down-to-earth. Strong-hearted, fiercely loyal. A soulmate. With her, Chris felt safe, equal. Loved for who he was—or at least, as close to who he was as he was willing to show her.

Almost immediately, he met Ali's family, and fell in love with them, too. Her father, Graham, was English by birth. He'd gone from private school to the British army, and had been tempted to make that his career, become a marksman. Instead, he went to law school, then joined his uncle's firm in London, Worley & Worley. That's where he met his wife, Deirdre—she was a legal assistant. In the 1960s, when Graham was in his thirties, he and Deirdre moved to Toronto, and he helped build what is now McCarthy Tétrault, one of the city's most prestigious white-shoe law firms. Graham didn't strike Chris as a typical corporate lawyer, though—he was a talkative, warm, reachable guy, who recited Shakespeare into his late seventies, and wrote poetry. (He died of cancer in 2008.)

Ali's mother, Deirdre, a real estate agent, was creative, open and genuine, with a cheeky sense of humour. A visual person with great taste in interior design, she was a strong role model for Ali and her older sister, Amanda. Deirdre created an environment where everyone is equal, and no conversation is off limits. She was also a toucher and a hugger, and Chris was starved for that.

Amanda was also petite, only five feet tall. A corporate lawyer like her dad, she prepared to the nth degree, talked a mile a minute, and was never wrong. Judges loved her. She was the backbone of the family, a planner who took the long view. She was the first person they turned to for help or direction, and she was generous and supportive without imposing herself. She gave you her thoughts, but she wouldn't tell you what to do. Also, she loved a great party, and if a table appeared at the right moment, she'd dance on it.

The first evening Chris met the Worleys, he was dazzled. They laughed a lot. They teased each other. They had little comic routines: Graham would hand over his wallet, and his wife and daughters would extract his money and leave him with a loonie. They talked about law and literature and art. They discussed and they disagreed. They were warm, open, welcoming, as different from his family as fleece is from flint. He even loved their three-storey house—vertical, modern, it was the opposite of the horizontal bungalows of his youth. As dinner stretched late, it became obvious to everyone that Chris wasn't going to make the long drive home to Lorne Park, at the opposite end of the city.

He was nervous. He'd never stayed at a girl's house before. When Graham and Deirdre climbed the stairs to their bedroom, Chris and Ali lingered on the main floor for a minute, unsure of what to do. Suddenly a pair of pajamas came fluttering down from the upstairs landing, followed by a shrink-wrapped travel toothbrush. Graham called out, "You might need these." Ali and Chris cracked up. She'd brought dates home before. Her father had never done that.

In the morning, Deirdre presented Chris with a boiled egg in an egg cup—the first one he'd ever seen. When he tried to slice off the top, he massacred it, delighting the Worleys. He was in.

That was June. In July, Chris had his race accident, and in the fall, Ali went back to Trent. But they spent hours on the phone, and she visited on weekends. He didn't tell her about the switch. He kept hoping he wouldn't have to.

The following fall, Chris enrolled at Trent, too, as a geography major. He shared an apartment with two other guys, but ate most of his meals and spent most of his time with Ali. He still couldn't get on a racing bike, but he did a bit of mountain biking and running. It wasn't ideal. His switch was persistent. But he was managing.

The next summer, he took a course on satellite imaging. Computer-graphics technology was nascent; the equipment was first-generation Apple Macintoshes with small black-and-white screens. But the students had access to a Canadian government site in nearby Lindsay, and Chris could see that this was the future. He could also see a future for himself in graphic design. Ali graduated, Chris transferred to the Ontario College of Art (now the Ontario College of Art and Design) in Toronto, and he pretty much moved into the Worleys' downstairs guest bedroom.

Chris loved living in the Beach. For the Jacksons, going east "to the city" had felt like a major excursion. Physically and psychologically, the Beach was as far removed from Lorne Park as you could get in Toronto. The neighbourhood was in transition, from an art colony to something more gentrified. To Chris it felt alive, diverse. In Lorne Park, you had to drive everywhere. In the Beach, the street life was non-stop; you could walk to a hundred restaurants and stores. He loved the long boardwalks that spanned the sand beaches, and the proximity of the lake. He and Ali rented an apartment, a two-storey coach house on Waverley Road. To earn extra money, they were cater-waiters at black-tie parties.

Chris began waterskiing again, recreationally. He taught Ali to waterski, too, and marvelled at how quickly she picked it up. He bought mountain bikes for Ali and Amanda, and they took long rides together.

Chris and Graham started running together every morning. Graham would do ten or twelve kilometres along the boardwalk, and then Chris would peel off and do more. Afterward, they'd meet at the Goof, a diner that was a Beach institution. They'd sit on the round stools and eat fried egg sandwiches, and Graham would tell Chris stories about when he ran in a club with Roger Bannister. (When Bannister broke the four-minute mile, Graham was there; he could call up details about the wind and the weather like it was yesterday.)

Soon Chris and Graham began doing marathons together. They'd wake up before dawn, wrap their toes with deerskin cloth, and smear Vaseline everywhere they needed to put it. Graham's average time was 4:10; Chris would finish an hour earlier and wait for him near the finish line.

Graham taught Chris archery, and engaged him in intellectual discussions about literature and life. Though Graham worked hard, he never rose to the top of his firm. He preferred to spend the extra hours with his family. He was interested in Chris, and encouraged him to be interesting—to think for himself. Graham understood the world Chris had grown up in, because he'd struggled with a chilly father of his own. He treated Chris like the son he'd never had. And for the first time Chris had a father figure he could confide in.

Chris still wore his Lorne Park uniform—grey flannels, blue blazer—but he didn't have a suit. When he started lining up interviews for graphic design jobs, Graham took him to buy one. (Jim had never done that; Arlene had bought Chris's clothes.) They went to Honest Ed's Warehouse Restaurant, a classic red-meat parlour (now gone) near the financial district, where Graham bought him a steak and his first martini, $5.50 for a fishbowl of a drink. Chris was a typical endurance athlete, skinny as a stair rail; as always, the gin went straight to his head. After lunch, Graham took him to a side-street tailor, where he got measured for a grey wool suit, double-breasted. Graham went back to work and Chris staggered home. He didn't know if he was dizzy from the booze or from happiness. Probably both.

Emboldened by his new family, Chris began to wonder about his birth parents. Arlene had told him the basic facts, but who were they, really? Why did they give him up? One afternoon, he drove to Lorne Park to talk to Arlene. It was a Wednesday— laundry day—so he knew she'd be home. (He couldn't go on a Thursday. Thursday was grocery shopping day.) He brought up his adoption.

"Jim would say, 'You're our child and that's it,'" Arlene

replied. But she filled in a few more details, including the fact that Chris's uncle, David McKee, had arranged the adoption.

Chris spent two weeks processing this information. Then he asked to meet with David and Nancy, who still lived in Lorne Park, around the corner from Arlene and Jim. Chris and Ali drove across the city on a Sunday evening. He remembers the date, November 27, 1990. Nancy was waiting for them in the living room, a letter in her lap written on thin blue airmail paper. "We feel it's the right time to give this to you," she told Chris. "You're old enough. Do with it what you want." She'd kept it all these years. Arlene didn't know about it.

The letter was from Kathy Dooher, the older sister of Chris's birth mother, Tess. The return address in the corner of the envelope read Christchurch, New Zealand. The letter was dated ten days after Chris's birth. In it, Kathy thanked David for taking such good care of her sister.

By the time Chris and Ali got back to their apartment, it was 11:30 p.m. They sat looking at each other, the letter on the little square table between them. "This is my ticket to finding my mother," Chris said. "Let's see if there's a K.A. Dooher in Christchurch." They phoned New Zealand directory assistance. The operator couldn't find one, and Chris hung up. He thought a minute, then dialed back to see if there was a K.A. Dooher anywhere in the country.

The same operator answered. She stayed on the line with Chris, trying every city in New Zealand. They found one hit: Kathy Dooher, in Dunedin. All of a sudden, this became real.

"We have a number now," Chris said to Ali. "What do we do about this?" He felt shaky, almost sick. By now it was 1:30 a.m. "Ali, you call her," Chris pleaded. "I can't."

Ali dialed. The phone rang. Panicked, she hung up. She and Chris took a few deep breaths. "Let's be mature about this," Chris remembers saying. Ali phoned again. A young man answered (Chris didn't know it, but it was his cousin Matthew). Ali said, "I'm calling from Canada, looking for K.A. Dooher." Matthew said, "One moment please." They could hear what sounded like a family party in the background.

A woman came on the line. "This is Kathy Dooher," she said.

"I'm sitting here with your sister's son," Ali said.

Kathy asked to speak to him. Chris got on the line. Kathy asked him a few basic questions, then said, "We'll be in touch shortly," and signed off.

Too wired to sleep, Chris and Ali were still talking when their phone rang at 2:30 a.m. It was Kathy. "I've been in touch with my sister," she said. "She may call you." Chris hung up, feeling like a skeleton that had opened its own closet door.

At 4:30 a.m., the phone rang again. Tess was on the line. The first thing she asked: "What is your full name?" The second thing: "Do you have long eyelashes?"

Chris was staggered. All his life, people had commented on his eyelashes. Chris and Tess spoke for half an hour. He learned he had two half-sisters, Melanie and Katrina. He felt an immediate connection to Tess, which surprised him. Some part of him felt like he knew her, and that this conversation, now begun, could just continue on and on. He also realized he was in a kind of shock. He was twenty-four years old. He had no relationship to this person, this Kiwi voice. Yet she had borne him. The fairy tale Arlene had told him all his life had, in the space of one night, become a crashing reality. He didn't know how to feel, vibrating between, "She's my mother. She's not my mother."

Two weeks after they spoke on the phone, a letter from Tess arrived, dated December 7. It contained photos of Tess, of her days in Toronto, of Chris's birth father. Within six months, she'd sent him a duffel-bagful of material. She even knitted him a New Zealand wool ski sweater, two tones of blue with a white skier on the chest.

The next June, Tess and Kathy arrived in Toronto for a four-week visit. Chris rented a house for them at Queen and Silver Birch, not far from his place on Waverley. He'd done a little research at an adoption agency, so he was expecting emotional ups and downs; he knew that everyone would need their own space.

But he wasn't expecting the powerful recognition he felt when Tess wheeled her luggage cart through the double doors of Toronto airport's Terminal 3. Here was a five-foot-tall version of himself. Same hands, same face. Same movements, facial expressions. Nothing in his life to that point matched what that felt like—someone who shared his genes. He felt all his history as an adopted child, like a train slamming into a wall. He and

Ali exchanged hugs with Tess and Kathy and drove them to Silver Birch to settle in. As they drank tea and made small talk, Chris and Tess couldn't stop staring at each other. The last time she'd seen Chris was the day she'd handed him to Nancy McKee.

The next four weeks were wonderful and complicated, thick with every kind of emotion. Chris felt confused: this is my mother, this is a stranger. He felt guilty, like he was betraying the family that had raised him, yet he also felt he had a right to know his mother. Tess was reliving her experiences in Toronto, and wondering all over again if she'd done the right thing. Kathy was emotional, too; she'd been a big part of this story.

Tess showed Chris all of "her" places—where she'd lived in Forest Hill, where she'd worked as a nanny when she first arrived. She told him that many nights, she used to cry herself to sleep. Chris wanted to know all of this, but sometimes it felt like a lot. Tess could be a bit clingy. Not only did she want to be around him all the time, she wanted to be in physical contact, touching him or patting him. She'd be on his doorstep at 8 a.m. for coffee. Ali joked that Tess was a bit like an old girlfriend.

Chris took Tess to his places, too—Lorne Park, his schools. She was impressed. "You know, you had it much better than your sisters did," she'd say. At first Chris would agree with her—certainly he'd been given many advantages. Gingerly, though, he started to share more of the sadness of his childhood. He was careful about it—even though his life with the Jacksons wasn't ideal, he wanted to reassure Tess that he knew she'd made the best choice she could have made, for the best reasons.

Three weeks into the visit, Chris and Ali took Tess and Kathy to Bala Manor, stopping in Collingwood along the way. He thought, "Tess can meet the Jacksons and see for herself what she thinks of them." Everyone was nervous. Chris felt like Tess's visit was one more thing he was "doing to" his family. In advance, Elizabeth had come right out and told him, "This will be a short visit." Chris supposed that Elizabeth was worried that Tess would invade her family space, and hurt her daughter Arlene.

All of the Jacksons were in Bala, plus some McKee cousins. To Chris's relief, everyone treated everyone cordially. There were cocktail hours, dinners, rounds of golf, boat tours. Chris took them to Clevelands House in the fastest ski boat (Kathy and Tess loved that) and they met some of his Muskoka friends, who told Tess stories. Chris showed off some of his waterskiing tricks, and taught Tess how to waterski, too.

Arlene and Tess managed to have a few mother-to-mother conversations (Arlene told Tess about the personal ads she'd placed in *The Globe and Mail*). Jim wasn't too interested in conversation, but he was always socially appropriate. Really, the surprise was Elizabeth and Cecil—they loved the peppery Kiwi ladies. The Bala visit stretched to five days.

Near the end of Tess's time in Toronto, she and Chris were tramping through the Caledon Hills. He was becoming attached to her. They shared the same feistiness, the same dislike of pretension. They'd be chatting about nothing much, and he'd be thinking, "This is my mother! She conceived me!" All his life he'd felt like something had been missing, and here was that thing, talking to him, offering him physical contact, wanting to connect with him. Now she was going away, and he didn't know when he'd see her again. During this conversation, an urgency kept rising in him, a need to tell Tess . . . something. He wanted her to know his true self, but at that point he had no words for it. He knew he needed her help, but he didn't know what to ask for. It felt like, "Rescue me."

Tess's emotions were roiling, too. On one of her last days with Chris, she told him she didn't want to go back home. She'd wanted to settle in Toronto all those years ago. The life she'd dreamed of wasn't in a dot-on-a-map New Zealand village. Chris was living the life she'd wanted. At that moment, Tess's daughter Melanie, who was fifteen, called. "When are you coming home, Mum?" she asked.

Chris felt freaked out. He knew the pain of being the unfavourite child. He didn't want Melanie or her sister Katrina to feel that. "Of course you need to go home," he told her. "Your husband and kids need you." When he and Ali dropped Tess and Kathy at the airport, Tess wept. She called him several times from the airplane, on her seat-back credit-card phone. "I'm missing you already," she said.

Tess had a powerful reaction to meeting the biological child she hadn't raised, and then leaving him again. A few days after arriving home in New Zealand, she left her family, travelling south to a hotel for three weeks to process everything. When she got back, she began to call Chris from a phone box in downtown Greymouth. At first she called a few times a week, then once a day. Soon she was phoning six or eight times a day, just to hear his voice on his voicemail. He could hear the rain in the background of her messages. She would ask him, repeatedly, "When are you coming home?"—meaning, to her.

During this same time, Arlene arrived at Chris's apartment one afternoon with her hands full. "I don't know how your father will feel about this," she warned. Then she handed him a black-and-white hospital photo, 8.5 by 11 inches. Baby Chris. He'd never seen the photo before. Arlene also handed him a yellow knitted baby blanket. He recognized that; he'd used it as a child. But with it were matching yellow baby clothes, which Tess had knitted. He'd never seen these things. Arlene had kept them hidden in a high cupboard his whole life.

It was all too much for Chris. He felt responsible for everyone. He wasn't close to the Jacksons, but he wasn't ready to alienate them entirely. He worried Tess had been traumatized by meeting him—that he was coming between her and her family. After a few months of intense contact, he told her they needed to take a break: no phone calls, no letters. He was processing a lot, and thought she needed to do the same. He even sent her information from the Children's Aid Society about birth parents reuniting with adult children. Months without contact stretched into years.

Eight years after Tess's visit, her daughter Katrina showed up in Toronto out of the blue, and stayed for almost a month with Chris and Ali. She wanted to know why Chris had cut ties. He tried to explain; she understood, somewhat. (Now she understands more.) Eventually, Chris and Tess got back in touch via email, but it would be an eventful two decades until they saw each other again.

In the Worleys, Chris now had a family who loved him, and a woman he adored. Chris and Ali did everything together. Friends used to call them "the twins." He loved her kindness, her sharp humour. He wanted to show her everything, experience everything with her. He'd spent so many years feeling like a chick that was trapped in its egg, banging on the shell, trying desperately to break out. Now he felt the shell was cracking, and he might be able to break out of himself. He asked her to marry him. She said yes.

As exciting as that was, it also filled him with fear. The person Ali knew was as close as anyone had ever come to the real Chris, but was still a projection. He was also racked with guilt and shame. He had this deep secret, which he could barely admit to himself. How could he possibly admit it to Ali, and risk losing everything he was just beginning to have?

One late afternoon in November, under the kind of iron-grey sky that is so unforgiving it feels like it will crush you, Chris was walking aimlessly. He found himself at the end of the road by the windy point of Ashbridges Bay. There was nothing but frigid water in front of him, hard pewter, even darker than the sky. "How can I keep hiding from Ali who I really am?" he thought, in despair. "I can't manage this anymore." Dusk was falling, along with flurries that looked like dirty rain. Southerly winds were driving waves onto the shore. Lake Ontario looked like an ocean, limitless. Chris felt a calmness steal into him. "It would be easy," he thought. "All your troubles would float away."

He waded into the water, chest deep. He didn't feel the cold, not at first. But his body wouldn't let him go further. He stood in the water for ten minutes, willing it to move. But he couldn't. By the time he came out, it was dark. The flurries had thickened; in the circular glow of the streetlights, the wet snowflakes looked like storms of moths. Chris saw no one. No one noticed his dripping wet clothes; no one saw his slight frame juddering with shivers or heard his teeth chatter. It was like being a ghost.

Throughout the time that Ali and Chris lived together, they would occasionally see the Jacksons—a dinner in Lorne Park, the odd weekend at Bala Manor. Ali never warmed to the Jacksons, however. She thought Jim was a bully, and found the extended family too patriarchal. One weekend at Bala, Arlene summoned Ali into the kitchen where the women were cutting pans of dessert squares. Through the window, Ali could see the men on the lawn, enjoying cocktails. Elizabeth corrected Ali's cutting technique once, then a second time. The third time, Ali put down her knife. "Perhaps it's better if you do it yourself," she said calmly, and walked outside. In all the time they were together, Ali and Chris had the Jacksons over to their place exactly once.

So it was a bolt from the blue when, in 1992, Jim contacted Chris: His signage firm, Display Signs, needed a production manager. Would Chris like the job? Chris said yes, but soon regretted it. He was stronger, but not strong enough to deal with Jim. Every morning he would drive from the Beach to Pantera Drive, just south of the Toronto airport, feeling sick with dread.

Chris enjoyed the job itself: being the liaison between the clients—including Skydome, the CN Tower, and Copps Coliseum—and the manufacturing team. He liked designing way-finding signage. But he loathed the way Jim treated everyone, from Jim's older brother Frank, Chris's uncle, who was a full partner in the firm, on down. As always, Jim behaved like the captain of the ship. When someone displeased him, he'd tear a strip off them, loudly, in front of fifty other employees.

On the day before Chris's wedding, a Thursday, the staff—many of whom had known him since he was in diapers—threw him a party. Afterward, around 2:30 p.m., Chris stuck his head into Jim's office. "Everything's in good shape," he said. "I'm off now to pick up my suit for tomorrow."

Jim looked up. "You're not going anywhere," he said. Chris began to protest. Jim shouted, "If you leave now you're fired." Everyone in the outer office was staring.

Chris fought to hold back tears. "Maybe you've forgotten, tomorrow is the most important day of my life," he said. Then he forced himself to say "Please don't come. I don't want you to come." Jim merely repeated his warning: "If you leave, you're done here."

Chris walked through the office, his face burning. He got into his car. Just as he put it in gear, his father's assistant of thirty-five years, Norma Humphries, ran up to him. She was in tears. She reached into the car and gave him a hug. "I want you to forget about that and enjoy your day," she said. (Chris never forgot her kindness. Her house was on one of Chris's cycling routes, and from the day she retired until the day she died, he would often stop by on a ride and check on her.)

The wedding went off as scheduled on October 1, 1993, a Friday evening. It was a lovely, traditional affair at the Vaughan Estate in Sunnybrook Park, a grand stone building surrounded by late-blooming gardens. Some of Chris's waterskiing friends arrived towing a ski boat filled with flowers behind their car. Tess wasn't there, but Ali had written to her, and Tess had sent a beautiful telegram, which someone read aloud. Jim did come, of course. How could he not? Many of his friends were there.

Let's stop here and ask the obvious question: How could Chris go through with a wedding? Wasn't this a betrayal of Ali, the woman he loved? Many people have asked Ali over the years—"How could he not tell you?" They feel outraged for her. She tries not to. There's no point, she says. He wasn't capable of telling her. Not then.

So what was Chris thinking? He was in turmoil, but he'd been that way since he was four. He thought this was what his life was, the way it would always be. He thought he could keep it under control, coexist with it. Many times he'd begun to tell Ali, but couldn't go through with it. And he wanted to marry her. He wanted to live happily ever after with her.

When he saw Ali walking down the aisle in her beautiful white gown, Chris said to himself, "Okay, it's all going to go away now. That's my bride. I'll wake up tomorrow, and all that pain will be gone."

CHAPTER FOUR

Becoming Kristen

« « « « « • » » » » »

For the next seven years, Chris did everything he could to keep that pain at bay. He and Ali lived as husband and wife. In all that time, only one small event, which she immediately filed in the furthest corner of her mind and has never told anyone, indicated that anything was awry. Ali became a massage therapist. Chris went back to work for Jim; as per usual, they never discussed the firing incident. When Jim sold the company in 1995, he walked away with millions, but gave his adopted son two weeks' severance. Chris went freelance, doing computer design from his home. The work was detail-oriented and absorbing. When Amanda got married to Mark Overbury at the Toronto Golf Club, Chris was one of Mark's groomsmen.

Of all the people in Chris's life, Elizabeth may have come the closest to sensing his diversity. When she died in the summer of 1997, at age seventy-eight, he was the last person she spoke to. Just before she died, she'd been scheduled to have heart surgery at St. Michael's Hospital in Toronto, and Chris had been with her when she checked in. But two days later, without telling anyone, she checked herself out and hired a taxi to drive her the two hours to Bala. Frantic, Chris finally got her on the phone. "I needed to take care of your grandfather," was all she said.

Two days later, on a Friday night, Chris drove north. When he pulled into his usual parking spot at Bala Manor, he noticed the bathroom light was off. This was unusual—Elizabeth always stayed up until eleven to take her heart pill. But he didn't want to wake her to ask. The next morning, he walked into the living room. The sun was shining in through the big windows looking over Bala Bay, and Elizabeth was in her easy chair at the far end of the room. But instead of her usual impeccable outfit, she was still wearing her nightie. Chris sprinted across the room and knelt beside her. "I'm having trouble breathing," she said.

Chris pulled her up out of her chair and into a hug, then moved around her so he was supporting her from behind. Together, they shuffled through the living and dining rooms, and down the hall to her bedroom. He got her a glass of water and ran to the next cabin, where the telephone and address book were, to phone her doctor in Bracebridge. He also phoned his uncle, David McKee, who called an ambulance.

When Chris ran back to the big house, he found the door locked. He dashed around and tried the other doors—all locked. Cecil had locked them. He could see that Elizabeth was dying; in his panic, he somehow believed this would keep her with him. He didn't open them until the ambulance arrived. The EMTs strapped Elizabeth to a gurney and covered her with orange blankets. Cecil leaned over for what turned out to be their last kiss. As they wheeled Elizabeth out of the room, Chris could see her eyes following the family photos lined up along the walls.

He wanted to ride in the ambulance, but Elizabeth said no. "I want you to stay here and enjoy the day," she said. "I woke up this morning and I was worried about you." Those were her last words. On route to the hospital, she went into cardiac arrest and fell into a coma. She died twenty-four hours later. Afterward, her family would discover that she'd socked away $50,000 in a secret account to help her grandchildren. It helped pay for medical school for one of Chris's cousins.

Soon after the funeral, Arlene and Chris found themselves alone in the kitchen at Bala Manor. Arlene asked Chris what Elizabeth's last words were. He told her, and her eyes filled. It was the first time he had ever seen his mother cry. He didn't sense that she was crying for Elizabeth, though. He wondered if she'd felt a stab of guilt—perhaps Elizabeth's words of concern for Chris pointed out Arlene's lack of it. Then he realized he didn't know why Arlene was crying, because he didn't know her as a person. If this were one of the Worleys crying, Chris would know why, or he would ask and they'd talk about it. But he wasn't privy to Arlene's emotional life. That was a strange feeling, to realize how little he knew his own mother.

In 1999, Chris was sitting in the Newark Airport waiting for a flight home when, out of nowhere, he started to hyperventilate. He'd landed a lucrative contract to design Pepsi concessions for the Silver City movie theatre chain. Pepsi had flown him to New York to do a presentation. He'd been a hit. But now, in the airport, the world was swirling in and out of focus. He broke into a sweat. His heart was pounding so hard, he felt sure it would seize.

He phoned Ali. "I don't know what this is," he said, "but I'm having a breakdown." She calmed him down enough that he was able to board his plane. During the flight, he repeated to himself over and over, "You'll be okay, you'll be okay."

Safely home, he realized what was happening. The glass wall that he had built between his real self and his life was finally shattering. He was thirty-four. His switch had been flipping for thirty years. It had now flipped for good. Chris's brain, his whole body, was saying, "That's it. You can't go on like this. You can't hide who you are anymore."

A few days later, on a Wednesday, he phoned Amanda. "Can I come talk to you on Saturday, privately?" he asked. He needed a few days to firm up his resolve.

Tentatively, he did an online search for psychiatrists or

psychologists who were experts in gender issues. (He realized he didn't even know the difference between a psychologist and a psychiatrist; that's how removed he'd been from the subject of mental health.) He was frightened. He was finally admitting to himself who he was. But what about Ali? (He told her he was having panic attacks.) What would happen to his design career? And what about his future in sport? He had so much invested in that. Sport had kept him alive. How could he go on if he lost it? It felt like he had stepped out of bed in the morning to find that the floor wasn't there. He could hardly stop crying.

On Thursday, he met with a young, female University of Toronto psychologist who was affiliated with the Clarke Institute of Psychiatry. At the time, the Clarke was Toronto's premiere centre for people with gender issues. Chris had no way of knowing that it would soon be widely discredited, nicknamed "Jurassic Clarke" for its regressive ideas and treatment policies. (The institute eventually changed its name to the Centre for Addiction and Mental Health, or CAMH, to distance itself from its flawed past.)

Unfortunately, the psychologist was new at her job. She didn't fully grasp the distress Chris was in. She threw words at him—"transgender, LGBT, queer identity, transsexualism"—words his family had never spoken, words he'd never allowed himself to think.

"You don't know who I am; this doesn't happen in my world," Chris told her.

When she replied, "This *is* who you are," he felt dread, not relief.

That Saturday, Chris arrived at Amanda's house at 9 a.m. and didn't leave until 3 p.m.. He cried for two full hours before he could begin to speak. When he finally did, he could only utter a few sentences at a time. What happened in Newark. His hiding places in Bala Manor. His three-decade story came out in shards, like glass—jagged pieces of pain.

Amanda simply listened. When Chris finally ran out of words, he swore her to secrecy. He could imagine only one outcome: everything he loved would disappear. Ali would leave him. He'd lose the Worleys. Though the Jacksons were mostly out of his life, he still saw people from his platinum triangle. They would never understand. He needed Amanda's help to strategize.

For the next eight months, Amanda kept Chris's secret. It wasn't easy. She hated not being open with her family. Her husband, Mark, knew she was keeping a secret, but didn't know what it was; it caused some tension between them. She suffered sleepless nights. Chris called her often, and often in a panic. She was constantly meeting him at a Starbucks on Queen Street, or going for walks. She tried to listen, but she had no expertise in this area, and he was stuck in a loop, repeating the same mantra of panic: "Why do I have to be this way? No one is going to like me. I can't leave the house. I can't be with people. Ali will leave me." Amanda would talk him off the ledge—"You're a good person. This is not something you've done to yourself. It's just the way you are"—and the next day Chris would call again. They'd have the same conversation they had yesterday, and last week. Amanda kept urging him to reveal himself to more people, so more people could help him.

Ali knew something was terribly wrong. She had fallen in love with Chris's energy, his zest for life. Now the brilliance had faded from his blue eyes. He'd snap at her. He'd storm around in silence. She begged him to talk to her about whatever it was. He wasn't ready.

For a while, Chris continued to see the young psychologist. Though she observed him more than she helped him, she was the only other person he could talk to. He kind of overdosed on it—not unlike the way he'd dived headfirst into sport. In no time, he had racked up $10,000 in bills.

He learned that his switch had a name: gender dysphoria, defined as "the condition of feeling one's emotional and psychological identity as male or female to be opposite to one's biological sex." That felt right to him, but it didn't make him feel better. Instead, he was feeling worse and worse. Time and again, he'd go to the internet for information and find statements from doctors that read like this: "If you transition, you'll likely lose your job, your family and your social network. But you must do it, to survive." Who on Earth could read that and not panic?

Eventually, Amanda contacted a legal expert who dealt with gender issues. That expert recommended the Clarke. At this point in time, the Clarke was run by Ray Blanchard and

Kenneth Zucker, who believed that homosexuals and trans-gendered people needed to be "reformed." Funded by the Christian right, they were doing tests that bundled people with gender issues into the same category as sexual offenders and the mentally ill. (The DSM—*The Diagnostic and Statistical Manual of Mental Disorders*—did the same, up until the fifth edition.) Their protocol was, "Go buy a wig, leave your wife, and move to Church Street [Toronto's gay village]. Live for two years as the opposite gender. Then maybe we'll give you some hormones."

They forced an exterior change—made people cross-dress—without any hormonal support or consideration for the physiological or mental health of the trans person. In 1989, Blanchard also coined the term "autogynephilia" (now discredited), which he described as "a man's tendency to be sexually aroused by the thought or image of himself as a woman." Blanchard believed that any man who said he was transgendered was in fact a gay man who couldn't accept his homosexuality (and vice versa for women). He believed it was "easier" for such a person to assume the opposite gender because it was so hard to be gay.

If Chris had been born twenty years later, his story would be different. Generally speaking, medical professionals in the Western world, including Blanchard, now support gender transition as an appropriate and beneficial practice. But in the year 2000, gender issues weren't as widely known or discussed as they are today.

Amanda accompanied Chris to the old Clarke building at College and Spadina, to his first appointment at the gender clinic. He met with Maxine Petersen, a sixtysomething staff therapist and a trans woman.

Chris balked. Here he was, speaking to the first transgendered person he'd ever met—a tall, broad, large-handed person in a long, red wig—but she was echoing Blanchard's beliefs about transgendered men, and describing Chris's present and future in bleak, unhelpful terms. (Petersen resigned in 2003, when Blanchard did.)

Next, he met with Dr. Robert Dickey, chief psychiatrist at the gender clinic. Dickey sat Chris down in a tiny white room flooded with light, and pelted him with questions. He asked about Chris's sexuality (Chris was mortified; answering such personal questions was anathema to him). He asked about Chris's behaviours: Was he cross-dressing and handling women's objects to soothe his anxieties? Yes. Was it disrupting his daily life? Yes. Did he have to excuse himself from things and rush off to soothe himself? Yes. Did it cause him anxiety? Yes. Hearing it out loud, saying it out loud, Chris felt like he was in a nightmare.

Dickey declared, "Science is showing us that this is who you are, a transgendered person. And you're realizing who you are."

He reached out and grabbed Chris's hands and said, by way of reassurance, "You have small hands, a small frame. You'll transition well."

The blood was roaring in Chris's ears. "This can't be me, this can't be me," he thought. He felt like he'd been holding up a boulder and had turned to people for help, only to watch them drop it on him instead. Given how rigidly he'd been raised, Chris felt stripped bare. He felt this was the end of hope.

A few days after meeting with Dickey, Chris finally told Ali the whole story. She held him. She told him she loved him. But inside, she thought, "Ohhhhhhh." She recalled the incident that she'd filed away and vowed to keep secret. Now it made sense. To Chris's immense relief, Ali told him she accepted him and loved him. But in a flash, her memories, her vision of her life, and her future plans rearranged themselves.

Despite Ali's immense empathy—or perhaps because of it, because he felt so guilty and ashamed; Chris's emotional state was far from clear—Chris again surrendered to his heartsickness. Around six-thirty one evening, when Ali was out and the sky was darkening, he tied a sheet into a noose. He went to the top of the stairs of their coach house, where the landing was like a balcony. He fastened the sheet to the banister rail and slipped the loop over his neck.

He didn't jump right away. He stood at the edge for a few moments, swaying in the noose, steeling himself for what he was about to do. For so long, he'd been fighting his diversity as if it were a choice. He was tired of fighting. He honestly felt everyone would be happier if he simply disappeared. Again, a sense of peace, almost euphoria, washed over him. He leaned into the sheet so hard, he lost consciousness. If Ali hadn't come home just when she did, it would have been too late. She rushed up the stairs and cut him loose.

Obviously, Chris wasn't getting the help he needed. Ali made him promise to fire his psychologist at his next appointment and came with him to see that he did.

Amanda went back to her legal-medical network and found Chris a new doctor: Samuel Malcolmson, a psychiatrist in his early sixties who had recently moved from the Clarke to an independent practice at Bloor and Church. Ten years later, in 2009, Malcolmson would lose his licence after pleading no contest to allegations of sexual abuse of a patient, and to "disgraceful, dishonourable and unprofessional conduct," after having a sexual affair and fathering a child with a patient. But when Chris met him, he was one of Ontario's most prominent and respected psychiatrists, and the first one who really helped him.

At this point, Chris was doing freelance design for a software development company. But projects that would normally take him a few hours were taking days. He would stare blankly at the screen, unable to see the steps he needed to take to complete his tasks. At home, he was talking to Ali and Amanda on a loop, "Why did this happen to me? How can I live this way?" Malcolmson knew that before tackling other issues, he had to bring Chris's anxiety and depression down to manageable levels.

Chris began seeing Malcolmson weekly. The doctor prescribed a selective serotonin reuptake inhibitor (SSRI), a class of drug typically used to treat anxiety and depression. Not every SSRI works for every person; the right one can be found only through trial and error. The first one Chris tried almost killed him (accidentally, due to a side effect). One morning not long after he began the medication, he was riding his mountain bike on a trail that runs along the Don River. He blacked out, tumbled nearly five metres down a slope, and fell into the water. Two riders going in the opposite direction saw him fall and rescued him. "It was the weirdest thing," they told him. "You were riding along and you just disappeared." He broke three ribs.

Malcolmson switched Chris to Zoloft. That was a new beginning. For the first time in years, Chris felt clear, as if a sliding door had suddenly opened and he'd walked through it. His anxiety eased. The fog in his mind dispersed. "Okay," he thought. "This is okay."

Not long into Chris's therapy, Jim and Arlene phoned him. Ali, who kept in sporadic touch with Arlene, had told her the bare minimum: that Chris was depressed and getting help. "We want to meet your therapist," they said. "We want to tell him our side of the story." To Chris, they seemed more concerned about what he might be telling his doctor than they were about his mental health. When Chris told Malcolmson about the call, the doctor laughed.

For the next two years, Chris saw Malcolmson once or twice a week for talk therapy. The doctor had walked away from the Clarke because he knew their rigid protocol for trans patients was wrong-headed. He allowed Chris to progress at his own pace.

Chris felt more functional, more organized. He wasn't less frightened, but he had some calm, some balance. He was sleeping better, gaining a little weight. His anxiety eased. Though his initial sessions with Malcolmson focused on Chris's gender issues, discussing his family soon became equally important. This big, scary idea—his gender diversity—became just one part of understanding himself in the full context of his life.

The heavy lead dome Chris had been living under lifted. But persistent fears remained. He'd figured out a way to pass, to be liked. He was terrified of losing that. He came to realize that he'd attempted suicide that third time because one last bit of himself was still fighting the truth. Now he had to admit it. The task ahead of him was massive, but he had to do it. He had to live as a trans person, or die.

This was the turning point. That was the moment Chris stopped holding his breath, and Kristen—me, I, the *real* me—began to breathe.

CHAPTER FIVE

Transitions

《 《 《 · 》 》 》

Some people think transitioning is easy: you take some hormones, change your wardrobe, restyle your hair. Maybe you have surgery, maybe not. But instantly you're comfortable in your new life. That's the way it looks on TV, right?

Those people are mistaken. Transitioning is a slow process, not just physiologically, but mentally and psychologically. Chris's—mine—took five years.

My next step was telling Deirdre. She and Graham had sold their Beach house and moved to a condo on St. Clair Avenue in Forest Hill. Ali, Amanda and I met Deirdre there for lunch. She could not have been kinder. She told me she loved me, and that I would always be part of the family. Privately, she was deeply worried about Ali. Ali was staying married to me—what did that mean for her? What was she giving up? But Ali coped by pushing aside all doubts and forging ahead, so Deirdre did the same.

Telling Graham was harder: he was the dad I'd always longed for, and we'd become so close. I arranged to have dinner alone with him at the condo. It took me a while to utter the first sentence: "I need to tell you what's going on." I told him I'd been feeling suicidal, but I was getting professional help. I wanted to show him that I was taking control, so he wouldn't be worried. Finally I said, "I'm dealing with gender dysphoria." I explained what that was, and how it was affecting me.

Graham didn't blink. He said, "I love you unconditionally, and I will help you with this." Later, he told his wife and daughters, "If someone had driven a Mack truck through the wall, I wouldn't have been as surprised." But to me, he said, "We're a family." When he hugged me, my relief was overwhelming.

I didn't tell Arlene or Jim. Ali did tell Jennifer, and I suppose she passed on the news. But I never heard from any of them. Neither my uncle, David McKee, nor my godfather, Bill Sloan (a senior executive at Arthur Andersen), ever picked up the phone to see how I was, either. In fact, once or twice when I ran into them on the street, they simply looked away. I did phone Jonathan, who was living in Colorado. He sounded panicked at the news. That phone call—over twenty years ago—was the last time we spoke. I also phoned Tess to tell her. I was hoping this would explain to her, at least partly, why I'd been out of contact for so long. But her reaction disappointed me. "That doesn't happen in our family," she said. All I could say was, "Okay." (To her credit, after that first call, Tess decided to educate herself about gender dysphoria and trans issues. When we finally got back in touch, she was much more open and accepting.)

When it came to other people in my life, I developed a schedule: once or twice a week, I phoned someone, asked if I could meet them privately, and told them. I did this with my closest friends first, and then radiated outward in concentric social circles. Almost everyone was kind in the moment. But it was stressful. It exhausted me. Every night after work, I'd come home and collapse on the sofa for two hours, often in the middle of dinner. Deirdre remembers me crying a lot. Sometimes I wanted to take it all back. Especially since, as the months and years wore on, Ali and I could feel friends falling away. It was nothing overt—they just stopped inviting us to things. They stopped returning calls. I landed fewer and fewer design contracts. Firms didn't openly discriminate—it was just easier for them to hire someone else.

Another person I did not tell was Hugh Walters, my birth father. Around 2003, I decided to search for him.

Tess wasn't in contact with him, and I wanted to protect her. But I was learning a lot about genetics, and I wanted to fill in that part of my story.

Graham's only sibling, his younger brother, Robert Worley, lived in the UK, where he worked for the British government. He was a bit of a family-history sleuth. Graham asked him to dig up information on Hugh. Six months later, Robert sent Graham a complete dossier in a pink folder, including a certificate that read "Birth: illegitimate." That's me, I thought. The power of words.

Hugh was living in Cleveland, Ohio, doing insurance work for Lloyds of London on Great Lakes ships. He was married to a woman named Susan (not her real name), and they had three children together. Robert sent Hugh a letter, and Hugh sent one back that said, in essence, "Yes, I'm the guy." Then Robert phoned Hugh in Cleveland, for final confirmation. Hugh said he didn't want to discuss this while he was home. Susan didn't know about Tess, she certainly didn't know about me, and he wasn't ready to tell her yet. But he gave Robert his contact information, which Robert passed on to me.

As happy as I was to have made contact with Tess, I'd learned from that experience to take my time, process what it means to me, how it fits into the puzzle of my life. I took a week or two to mull it over, and then let Robert know I was ready. He arranged a time for me to phone Hugh at the end of the work day in his Cleveland office. Hugh answered in a hearty Welsh voice. He asked how I was, and about Tess. I felt protective of her, so I didn't say much. He asked where I lived, what I did for a living. We spoke for about twenty minutes. I'd felt connected to Tess just hearing her voice, but I didn't feel that with Hugh. Over the next few months, he phoned me three or four more times, always from his car or office.

Eventually, we decided to meet. First, Hugh took Susan to their cottage and told her the story. Her reaction: "How do we know this Chris person is telling the truth?" Hugh said there were "many tears," and that Susan wouldn't let him tell their children. But on a rainy, cold late-fall weekend, Ali and I drove to a roadside motel in Dunkirk, New York, a small town we picked as a midpoint between Cleveland and Toronto.

Though I was pretty far along in my transition to Kristen, I decided to meet Hugh as Chris. It felt like a disguise, but Hugh was a conservative Catholic, and I wanted to make things as easy as possible. When you're transitioning, you learn it's better to bring people along with you, however slowly. Otherwise they run away. I didn't want Hugh to do that.

Hugh and Susan got there first. When Ali and I entered the lobby, we saw Hugh, alone, sitting in a chair. He was weathered-looking, with a big head of hair. We had a little chat in the lobby—"How do you do, complete stranger who fathered me?"—and then checked in.

Hugh and Susan wanted to meet in their room. When Ali and I arrived, Susan was sitting sideways on the bed, arms crossed, watching a cop show on TV. She might as well have worn signs: "Don't get too close" and "I'm in charge here." She never got up off the bed.

During the weekend, Hugh and I took a few walks together; he asked a few questions about me. But he was always itchy to get back to Susan. Afterward he wrote me, asking, "Can you be nice to Susan?" I wrote back, "I can't manage your situation with her. You need to do that. I'm just trying to know my father."

The next time we spoke, he told me Susan wanted us to take blood tests. "Maybe Tess is lying to Chris," she'd suggested.

I told Hugh, "This is going the wrong way. You're not going to do this to Tess, or to me. Stand up for yourself."

Hugh remained in my life, long-distance, for about two years. He said he wanted to have a relationship with me, but there were always conditions. Gradually, I stopped contacting him. He wrote to me for a while, asking me what happened. I knew what it was: I'd met Hugh in disguise, as Chris. But I never felt enough of an emotional connection to tell him that. Soon enough he, too, stopped trying.

———

Brain-sex science is still considered a new field. Researchers have been investigating it since the 1980s but medical schools are only beginning to teach it. As I was going through my transition, I sought out and sent emails to doctors and researchers who could explain it to me. I established a relationship with one of the world's leading brain scientists, Dr. Dick Swaab, a professor of neurobiology at the University of Amsterdam and the team leader of its neuropsychiatric disorders group. Over our long correspondence, he explained his findings to me: that both gender identity (the feeling of being female or male) and sexual orientation (being hetero-, homo- or bisexual) are programmed in the brain before birth. They're encoded in the very structure of the brain. I'll do my best to explain this in layperson's terms.

The first thing you need to know is that every human has both estrogen and testosterone (also known as androgen). The common belief is that testosterone is the male hormone, and estrogen the female, but that's not correct. The ovaries and the testicles make both, and both are needed for human health.

At conception, every fetus is physiologically female, whether its chromosomes are XX (what we think of as female), XY (what we think of as male), or one of the twenty-seven variants found in human development, such as XXY (though variants are rare, they occur more often than most people realize). At ten weeks' gestation, sex organs begin to form: The fetus makes either ovaries or testicles. (That's why testicles need to "drop": they're created in the same place as ovaries.) If there's a Y chromosome, it stimulates the testicles to produce more testosterone, which signals the body to make the vulva into a penis.

In the average person, the brain and the body develop in the same direction. If the fetus is XX, it continues developing as a female; the ovaries send the brain a wash of estrogen that tells the brain it's female, and the brain begins forming cellular-level structures typical of female development. Put simply, some areas of the brain become larger than others and become strongly connected to other brain areas. (These cellular-level structures are not visible to the human eye, but they are visible under a microscope.) Similarly, if the fetus is XY, the testes send a wash of testosterone to tell the brain it's male, and the brain begins forming structures and connections typical of male development. Scientists call those structures and connections "organizing effects." Organizing effects are permanent. You cannot change them.

So, in the case of anyone who is intersex or trans-gendered, the chromosomes told one thing to the body without communicating that thing to the brain. In Chris's case, his Y chromosome directed his body to develop into a male. But his testes didn't send increased testosterone to his brain, so his brain structures and connections didn't become masculinized.

In puberty, your sexual organs send another wash of hormones, either estrogen or testosterone, to activate the organizing effects that were built in the brain in the womb. But if those organizing effects weren't built—by that sex-related wash of hormones—they can't be activated.

Dr. Swaab and his team learned all this by studying brains postmortem. Back in the 1980s, they began seeing and documenting how the organizing effects in XY brains differed from those in XX brains. In 1990, they found the first structural differences in the brains of XY homosexuals as compared to XY heterosexuals. Five years later, they found the first evidence of the reversal of sex differences in the brains of transgendered people. These findings have been widely accepted by gender scientists. And they've been accepted legally—for example, the European Court in Brussels used them in their ruling that allows trans people to change their birth certificates and passports.

In one of our phone calls, Dr. Swaab stated his findings as bluntly as he could. "Sexuality and gender are programmed in the brain before birth," he told me. "They're not a choice. The choice is made for all of us in the womb. Everyone who knows the literature should by now agree on that. There is no reason to think that after birth, society has any influence on our gender identity or sexual orientation. I know that in the United States there are places that try to make homosexuals into heterosexuals. The only result is there are more suicides."

But the process of brain-sex development is infinitely complex. In a fetus, a certain amount of testosterone or estrogen must be produced at the right moment. The brain areas involved must be developing in sync. The sensitivity of the nerve cells that accept the testosterone or estrogen should be neither too strong, nor too weak.

For instance, one variation, called androgen insensitivity syndrome, occurs because some XY fetuses have a small mutation in the protein that is the receptor for testosterone. When testosterone is brought to the brain cells, the receptor can't receive it. So the brain differentiates in the female direction.

Due to this infinite complexity, the variations that are present in all humans—body shape, skin colour, facial features, and so on—are also present in gender identity and sexual orientation. In other words, just as humans are not strictly only "athletic" or "uncoordinated," they are not strictly only male or female, but that and also everything in between. And they are not either heterosexual or homosexual, but also everything in between.

Socially, we understand this to some degree—we might, for example, call some girls "girly" and others "tomboys." But we're not taught to accept that gender itself has infinite variations. We're taught to think "girl" or "boy."

The science explains to me why, when I was around three years old, I was already struggling with who I was.

My body had built male organs, and society was conditioning me to fit into the mould it has constructed for boys. Society and the brain's organizing effects reinforce each other—think of how many parents will tell you that no matter how gender-neutral they try to be with their son, he is more interested in trucks than he is in dolls. Whether they mean to or not, they usually reinforce that preference—they give him more trucks and fewer dolls, and soon the dolls disappear. Now think about the Jacksons. It never occurred to them to even try to be gender-neutral with their children. Everything they gave and said to Chris reinforced his "boyness." But my brain hadn't built those male structures. That's why my switch flipped, and why that gender-confusion made me anxious and depressed.

Now imagine yourself at puberty. If you're an XX female, you expect your breasts to get larger; you expect your pubic hair to grow; you expect to get your period. (And even if you're eager for it to happen, it's still pretty weird when it does, right?) Now imagine Chris, who didn't feel like a male. Imagine my horror as body hair grew all over me, my voice deepened, and my penis got larger. My (female) hypothalamus wasn't prepared for the hormonal changes of a male. That's why in puberty, my switch-flipping became relentless. I didn't feel like I was becoming a man; it all felt so strange to me, I might as well have been becoming a werewolf.

———

There's no manual for transitioning. It's not like changing a light bulb. In Toronto in 2000, there were hundreds of endocrinologists, but perhaps four of them knew the ins and outs of gender reassignment, and were willing to take on patients. Sam Malcolmson connected me with one of them, a doctor who had a practice at Bay and Bloor. She set up a sensible, gradual hormone treatment plan to suppress my testosterone and increase my estrogen.

This is a crude analogy, but imagine you want a little more muscle definition. You don't start with hundred-pound barbells, you start with five-pound hand weights. You add reps. You get a little stronger. You increase to ten-pound weights. You add new exercises. And so on.

In a similar way, the hormones dictated my transition. The first change I noticed was relief. My hypothalamus was going, "Thank you! That's right! Get out of here, testosterone, you never belonged here. Come on in, estrogen, you're what I need." It was like having a drink when you've been thirsty for days. I felt euphoric. Very gradually, my pelvis widened, my skin softened, I grew breasts.

But as I said, it wasn't easy. Even though we were adjusting my hormones gradually, when your testosterone drops as your estrogen soars, your brain goes through a massive chemical change and adjustment. Along with relief and delight, you also feel depression, confusion, anxiety and doubt: "Why do I have to tell so-and-so?" "This is too difficult." "I'm scared to wear women's clothes in public. Can't I just wear them at home?"

Ali jokes (but isn't joking) that she married a man, raised a teenager, and ended up with a wife. By teenager, she's referring to my hormonal changes. For the first few years, she had to keep reminding herself how she'd felt as a teenager, and that I was basically hormone soup.

I didn't know how to look like a woman, so I tried to be a teenage girl. Ali had to teach me to dye my hair, to paint my nails. That must have been weird for her, but I couldn't think about that. I gave myself a goal—go to the Bay and buy women's underwear—and then agonized over it for days. When I finally started buying women's clothes, I went through what Deirdre calls my pink phase. I was sick of grey and blue. I wanted colour. Blouses, not shirts. Pastel socks. Ali kept steering me toward what she called the Ellen DeGeneres look— women's jeans or black pants, cashmere sweaters, cute flats. Graham called my attention to subtleties: "My dear, you need to relearn how to pick up an apple," he would say to me, or how to reach for the stem of a wine glass, or how to sit with my legs closed.

My first trip to a women's public washroom was an adventure. I was with Ali and Deirdre at the Sherway Gardens mall in Mississauga. Before I could go through that door, I had to sit in the concession area and steel myself. My heart was pounding. Would people glare at me? Would I cause a scene?

To make me laugh, Deirdre and Ali told me the ladies' room rules: Don't pee too hard. Suppress certain noises. No talking in the stall, talk at the sink only. (This was all new to me.) Then Deirdre dragged me in. "Whatever you do," she said, "your feet point forward!" (Meaning, sit—though I no longer had the equipment for standing.) Afterward, while I was washing my hands, two or three women came in, but they didn't give me a second glance. A small triumph, but an important one.

After the pink phase, I stuck mostly to unisex clothes, and didn't present as rigidly "male" or "female." Still, when Ali and I would walk down the street, a lot of people would stare. I expected that. (I was and still am surprised by the cruel things some people say, even in open-minded Toronto.) I wouldn't meet their eye. Ali would stare them down for me.

One particular day in the middle of my transition stands out. It was Easter, one of the first really sunny days of spring. The Beach was hopping. Ali and I were sitting on the steps of a church across from Kew Gardens. My hormones were doing their work, and my body was in mid-change. I was wearing a simple white T and jeans. This tall, bald, muscular guy walked by. Every inch of visible skin was tattooed. But passersby weren't staring at him. They were staring at me. He was a spectacle, but they knew what he was. He fit into the silo marked "male." No one could tell what I was. They were straining to identify me as either/or, because that's how we're socialized.

People stared at Ali, too—"What is she doing with That?" That was hard for her; she didn't choose this. As well, our acquaintances gossiped behind her back—"I didn't know Ali played for the other team." It wasn't any better when people asked us questions directly; that felt to us like prying.

Sometimes we would think, Why shouldn't we stay together? We love each other. Our marriage is about a lot more than sex. We want to keep our family intact. I'd suffered a lifetime of rigid conventions—why stick to one more? We saw that most relationships don't work out, regardless of gender orientation. Couldn't we be different? As well, imagine if your partner had an accident, became paralyzed, or got cancer. What I was going through wasn't that, but it felt like a kind of catastrophe. I needed Ali's help, and she wanted to help me.

Other times I could see how hard this was on her. Transitioning is narcissistic. You are self-obsessed. It has to be about you. I was in the battle of my life—I had to articulate the same fears, day in and day out, and Ali had to listen. I was polite to people all day. When I got home, I could be short-tempered, or a hollowed-out zombie, or a tearful mess, and she supported me unconditionally.

When I was too distressed to work, or when no one would hire me—the discrimination against gender-diverse people is staggering—she had to double down and massage that many more bodies. *Yes, therapy is expensive. I need it. Yes, electrolysis treatments cost $10,000. I need them.*

I know now that many nights, Ali would look at me and think, "I'm alone in this room, even though there's another person here." But she never said it aloud. And when she was at her wit's end, one day when she thought, "Whatever I do, it's never going to be enough," she went out and bought me Bella, a luscious black Labrador. Bella gave me a reason to get up every morning, even on the days I wanted to sleep forever, and to go outside when all I wanted to do was hide.

It's no exaggeration to say that Ali kept me alive. I don't call her my angel lightly. Amanda used to say to Ali, "Don't go down with the ship. Let's not lose two lives in this vortex." But what I was experiencing was so all-consuming, what else could she do? For years, Ali had a recurring dream: she and I would be walking down a street, someone would shoot at me, and she'd throw her body in front of me and take the bullet. We didn't need therapy to figure that one out.

I needed her, so she was there. She would come home and find me in her pantyhose. She was uncomfortable with that, but she didn't want me to be uncomfortable, so she kept that to herself. She had to mourn a person who was still alive, who slept beside her every night. And I couldn't help her with that. I had to keep moving.

Here's a hard truth. I saw that Ali, this woman I loved, was doing everything she possibly could for me. And yet I still felt—often—that I was in this alone. No matter how valiantly Ali and her family tried to understand me, part of me was sure they never would. No matter how much they stuck by me, I couldn't shake the fear that every new step I took would be the last straw for them. As a cyclist, being selfish was essential to my training—"I'm sorry you're lonely, but I have to get up early/train all weekend/be away at races." Now I was transferring that selfishness to my transition. No matter how much others did for me, I'd internalized the idea that, at the end of the day, I was out there by myself.

On the Ides of March, 2004, I went through a full surgical transition. (Even if I wanted to, I couldn't forget that date, because the Worleys always send me bunches of tulips, with a card that reads "Happy Birthday.")

It took a lot to get there. My surgery wasn't covered by Ontario's health plan, so Ali and I had to raise the $30,000-plus that it cost. To be honest, I was still struggling to get and keep work, so it was mostly Ali. She and her friend Ardith Allen held a swim-a-thon; they spent numerous days, over several months, gliding back and forth in pools and raised $11,000. Graham and Deirdre handed us an envelope filled with traveller's cheques. Then one donor—who wants to stay anonymous—wrote us a massive cheque that took us over the top.

Graham and Deirdre swapped their usual time-share in Mexico for an apartment in Montreal, so Ali and Deirdre could stay with me a full month—from my surgery at the Centre Métropolitain de Chirurgie on the edge of the city, through my recovery in a special facility nearby.

I was excited. My doctor, Pierre Brassard, was the leading sex reassignment surgeon in North America; his patients came from around the world. (Coincidentally, he'd been a waterskier; he knew about Chris.) I had spent four years preparing myself for this, researching the science as rigorously as I'd trained in sports. I kept reminding myself that my brain and body would finally be aligned. But I was also scared. There was still a part of me that was Chris. I was ending his life.

The night before the surgery, the nurses handed me a razor and instructed me to prep the area. Ali was the one who shaved me. I can't imagine how strange and sorrowful that must have been for her. At one point I tried to lighten the mood. I turned to my roommate, Gwen (born Steven), and asked, "Would you like to see a picture of my dog?" Ali and Deirdre found that hilarious. (Gwen's family sounded a bit like mine. One day in Steven's boyhood, he was dancing on his dresser in girl's clothes. His dad, an OPP officer, walked in on him. His dad said only, "Dinner will be on the table in five minutes." The "ignore it and it will go away" school of thought. Gwen is now a filmmaker in Vancouver. We stay in touch.)

Then they gave me a sedative, and I got weepy. Ali and Deirdre held my hands, and we all cried a few tears for Chris.

On Tuesday morning, I was wheeled in for surgery. Twenty-four hours later, I woke up bandaged, groggy and heavily medicated. I was scared to look down at myself. The doctors forced me to, because I had to do a lot of self-care; I had to become very familiar with my new genitals. When I finally did look, I was so swollen I could hardly see anything.

On Wednesday, I had my first bath. (To heal, I had to bathe two to three times a day.) Looking down between my legs, part of me thought, "Cool!" while another part of me asked, "Where is it?" My brain had transitioned as far as it could. My body was in shock.

After I was discharged, I spent two weeks in a facility nearby, for people who'd just had gender reassignment surgery or are about to have it. Three specially designed meals a day, quiet, with time to think and heal. To protect our privacy, it's located on an island in a lake, down a long laneway and then over a bridge. It was under tight security. Visitors had to be buzzed in. If you weren't told where to find it, you'd never know it was there.

At the time, it was the only such place in Canada. (Eventually haters did manage to find it—it was fire-bombed in 2016.)

There were ten of us recuperating together—eight women and two men of all ages, who had come from all over the world, from different professional and cultural backgrounds. At thirty-five, I was the youngest. It was a strange time. First of all, I was pretty medicated. Secondly, my body was in shock. I didn't think, "Hurrah, I have a vagina, I'm a woman!" I was barely aware I had one for the first few days. I had to relearn what my genitals looked like. I had to relearn how to go to the bathroom.

I would go out for walks—ever the restless athlete—but no one else did. We shared meals together. We talked. The care wasn't psychological, it was convalescent. There were lessons about bathing, cleansing, preventing infections. I was swollen and massively black and blue. A caregiver handed me a vaginal dilator, a thin plastic shaft, and instructed me to insert it like a tampon nine times a day for forty-five minutes at a time. (You do the math. It fills up the day.) As the weeks go on, the dilators get thicker.

I didn't have to explain myself to anyone there, so that was a relief. But many of the patients were so alone. They were divorced, separated, cut off by their families and old friends. It was sobering. Ali and Deirdre tried to help them, too, and I mean help—cleaning up vomit, changing bandages. Ali even learned how to palpate my prostate (which remains after surgery). Amanda referred to them as Florence Nightingale and Mother Teresa. But every day when Ali and Deirdre left, I would worry that they'd never come back. In the mornings I'd stand in the foyer, my hand on the doorknob, so I could rush out the minute I saw them.

After they drove me home to Toronto, the work of transitioning continued, with absorbing new problems. Seven days in, I began experiencing terrible, raw pain, dead centre in my lower pelvis. I was waking up several times a night, drenched in sweat. Soon, I couldn't get out of bed. Deirdre and Ali drove me back to Quebec. I had an infection; my body was rejecting some of the external parts that had been made into internal parts. The surgeon had to go up through my vagina to correct it.

I'd been told that it would take me six months to heal. It was more like a year. The swelling persisted, as did the bruising. I spent months sitting on a donut. I had to do hours of dilation exercises every day, and will have to do some for the rest of my life. It took me a full six months to be comfortable with touching my body. I went into spontaneous menopause. I experienced a version of phantom limb syndrome—I kept having flashes of panic that my penis was still there. Very few family doctors knew how to care for transitioned bodies. We had to do a lot of doctor shopping, and even then, Ali had to teach my GP about my prostate.

The first time I went to a public swimming pool with Ali, Deirdre, Amanda, and Amanda's son Hartley, the women said to me, "Just watch what we do." But we were all sweating. Well, not Hartley. He provided comic relief. He was at the genital-discovery age. He went around the group: "I have a penis, and Mommy has a vagina, and Nanny has a vagina, and Aunt Ali has a vagina . . . and Auntie Kris has a vagina." We all sighed with relief at that one. Ali had to remind me not to talk too much, because my voice was still too deep; the minute I opened my mouth, everyone would look at me. I also took speech classes; the instructor sent me home with a breathing apparatus to teach me to raise the pitch of my voice.

One of the toughest adjustments, believe it or not, was peeing. A woman's urethra is smaller than a man's. As Chris, I could hold it. As Kristen, when I had to go, I had to GO. I had to relearn all my sensations and timing. No more peeing outside, behind a tree or over a bridge. It's not easy becoming a woman.

And of course, there was the emotional transition. I never regretted the surgery. It wasn't a choice, it was an imperative. But I still had to make peace with my past, reconcile where I came from. Until I was fifty years old, I really struggled with Christmas and birthdays. I would often bow out of celebrations with the Worleys at the last minute. It was stressful for them, never knowing if I would show up or not. Ali would leave me behind and carry on, but my absence was always a presence. All these years later, my emotional journey hasn't ended. Perhaps other trans people have an easier road, but I'm still walking mine.

The next step, changing my name and gender on all my legal documents, was downright Kafkaesque. Dr. Brassard had given me the affidavit that the Canadian government requires. But the people who worked at the various bureaus were often uninformed about how to deal with situations like mine. To change my driver's licence, I had to chase down my local MP, Maria Minto, for her signature. Ali had to educate a Revenue Canada officer about transgender issues. The passport office was the usual nightmare. By the time Census Canada knocked on our door, Ali had had it. She told them, "Sorry, Chris died."

I had spent a lot of time thinking about what my new name should be. For the four years I'd been transitioning, I'd been living as Kristen Jackson. I wanted to make it easy for people; they could still call me Kris. But after my surgery, I wanted a fresh start. I talked to Ali about changing my last name to Worley.

It was a radical idea. We were still married, after all. What would we be to each other now? I suggested we'd be sisters. She had to let that idea steep for a while. Eventually she brought it up with the rest of her family. They were receptive, but they had questions to work out.

Their close friends knew about me, but what would they say to acquaintances or business associates? And Deirdre blanched a little when she heard that I wanted my middle name to be Dawn. I wanted it to represent my new day. But Dawn is also Ali's middle name. Perhaps Deirdre thought I'd taken enough from her.

But the Worleys did what they always do: they rallied around me and held me up. They invited me to dinner at Amanda's. Gathered around the table, they said, "Kristen, you're a part of our family." From that day until now, they introduce me as Ali and Amanda's sister. Amanda's children call me Aunt Kristen.

About four months later, a big government envelope arrived at the Worley house. Ali, Deirdre, Graham and I opened it together. Out slid my birth certificate, driver's licence, health card. Kristen Dawn Worley. A legally born female.

If this were a movie, I would have burst into tears and hugged everyone, then fallen back in my chair with a smile, bathed in righteous satisfaction. But life isn't a movie. Yes, staring at the documents felt good. I said, "That's cool." But as with transition, the change didn't sink in overnight. Imagine if, on your thirty-eighth birthday, someone told you to forget who you've been and start life again from day one. I'd changed my name, my body, and my outward relationship to the rest of the world. But I hadn't really lived as Kristen yet. It would take a few more years to fully transition in my own mind. I put the birth certificate away in a drawer, and didn't look at it for a long time.

One change did happen quickly for me. I began to, and still do, wake up in the morning filled with excitement rather than dread. I liked getting dressed in my clothes. Wearing a scarf, crossing my legs, walking with a sway in my hips. It felt liberating to express that, and to interact with people as myself. I liked how much more mental space I had. Before, so much of my brain was occupied with hiding, covering, projecting, wondering, worrying. At last I was free to think about work, friends, family, current events, without the fog of who-am-I. I was excited to run with my dog, and think about breathing and stretching, without all those other nagging doubts. My identity was no longer circumscribed by the Jacksons, or limited to my sport, or preoccupied with my transitioning. After five years—after thirty-eight years—my identity was finally Kristen. I wanted to figure out who that was.

There was one thing I was still terrified to change: being married to Ali. You might think I was selfish, maybe even monstrously so. I wouldn't argue with you. But I was still so vulnerable, and Ali was so strong. I leaned on her for everything. She had co-created me. If she walked away now, I might dissolve. And for her part, she'd been helping me for so long; she'd invested her money, time, love and years. How could she get me this far, and then leave me before I was ready?

So we stayed together for seven more years. Seven. I know it wasn't easy for her. But she'd committed to taking care of me, and she honoured that commitment in ways visible and invisible. One example: in 2008, Graham was diagnosed with a rare bone cancer. In June, as he lay on his deathbed at the Sunnybrook Hospital, Ali gave up her place at his bedside so I could hold his hand for a while before he passed. She remembers thinking, "I've had him longer than Kristen has. I know what he means to her. She can have his last hour."

Sometimes, our situation was so odd it was almost funny. Graham's obituary listed three daughters. I over-heard people at his funeral asking one another, "Did you know they had a third child?" At one point that day, I was standing right beside Ali when an acquaintance asked her, "I haven't seen Christopher, where is he?" She looked around the room and said, "Oh, I don't know." I didn't say a word.

Other times, it was heart-wrenching. About a year before Graham died, Ali and I decided to try for a baby. She wanted to be a mother, and I wanted her to have everything she wanted. We decided we'd be co-mothers. A remarkable person, who I won't name, volunteered to be our sperm donor. We tried numerous times, and I won't go into the details. But in July, a month after Graham died, Ali found out she was pregnant. We were thrilled, but also anxious—How, really, were we going to do this?

Four months later, Ali had a miscarriage. We never tried again.

When Ali first found out she was pregnant, Amanda gave her a pair of Robeez, little leather baby shoes. After her miscarriage, she couldn't bring herself to throw them out. So she framed them in a shadow box, and hung it in her bedroom. Those shoes sum up her losses, great and small. They're still the first thing she sees when she wakes up.

By September 2010, Ali was staying out late, leaving home early. She finally told me: she'd fallen in love with a man named Michael. She was exhausted; she needed to find her own life again. I guess it was inevitable, but emotionally I felt betrayed. Our relationship was hardly conventional. I would have accepted an open marriage, but that's not what she wanted.

As she remembers it, I was angry. I'd call it frightened. This wasn't supposed to happen. I hadn't fallen out of love with her. She'd always promised she'd stay. She'd also been thinking about this a lot longer than I had, so I was emotionally well behind her.

Imagine the devastation of any divorce—you have to learn to live alone, support yourself alone—and then add my diversity to it. Throughout that long process of transition, I'd had someone to live with, share income with, talk to. Life on my own as a trans person would be very different. After we split, as far as society was concerned, Ali would be okay. Whereas I had no evidence to show that I would be. For a trans person alone, it's a big, scary world, filled with prejudice. There's a lot of suicide among trans people. I didn't want to be another statistic.

Ali understood this. She stuck around for several extra months. She moved out in May 2011.

Even our split wasn't free of black comedy. On our divorce application, my name didn't match the name on our marriage certificate. So who exactly was getting divorced? Ali spent many nights researching Ontario divorce laws; there was nothing about trans people at the time. Everyone assumes a same-sex family is a gay family, but we were proof that isn't always true. Ali spent seven long hours in a courthouse one day, waiting in lines, filling out forms and getting affidavits signed. Ticking the final box—the reason for divorce—she didn't want to blame my transition. She wrote the truth: "Irreconcilable differences."

For a few months after she moved out, Ali and I didn't contact each other, though she worried about me constantly. Amanda and Deirdre reassured me that we would always be family—they said that was never even a question—but at first I couldn't believe it. I retreated into my apartment, and stopped interacting with people. I lost weight. (Deirdre, concerned, sent me deliveries from Grocery Gateway.) I couldn't earn money. It was very, very hard, on all of us.

It took about two years for Ali and me to find our way into our current relationship: best friends. Sisters. Michael accepts my place in Ali's life. We all eat dinner together several nights a week. Ali and I are and likely will remain one another's most important person. People think relationships have to be binary: you're either married or divorced. Why can't people be intertwined differently? We're taught that divorce equals failure. But for Ali and me, it was the best thing we could do. Our relationship didn't fail. It evolved. We got to where we needed to be.

Everyone is fascinated by what happens when people behave badly. But I think it's much more interesting, much more moving, when people behave well. We can only behave well when we're open to it, when we embrace a natural evolution rather than restrict it or control it. Ali and I are a love story. It's not your typical love story. But it's the real thing.

Amanda's son was born in 2003, her daughter in 2005. They only knew me as Auntie Kris. From them, I'd only ever had unconditional love and acceptance: I'm just me, unburdened by any baggage. That was a gift. I was nervous about messing that up. But in 2016, I decided it was time to tell them the backstory. Nervously, I wrote them each a letter and gave them an article about me that had appeared in *Cycling* magazine. Amanda gave them the envelopes. They read.

"Mum, we already know," they said. For them, it was a non-event. They were interested to learn that I'd been married to Ali; they only knew me as the adopted sister. But the fact that they greeted the rest with a shrug? One of the happiest days of my life.

CHAPTER SIX

Becoming an Activist

« « « • » » »

Michelle Dumaresq, who's from the interior of British Columbia, arrived in the downhill mountain biking scene in 2001. The sport was well established in other countries, but it was new to Canada; the players were still establishing themselves. The media soon learned that Dumaresq is a transitioned XY female. The reaction was, well, reactionary: *How dare she?* I was in the middle of my transition then, and I was paying attention.

Most people in the world, sport overseers included, assume that XY people—people born in male bodies—will always be stronger than XX people, people born in female bodies. Never mind that transitioning changes male bodies into female ones, by changing one's body shape and musculature; let's leave that aside. Automatic XY dominance is simply not true on any level. After transitioning, I occasionally raced against the Canadian cyclist Clara Hughes, an XX female. She was four inches taller than me and thirty pounds heavier; she could out-ride me and often did. Serena Williams, the XX female tennis player, can whip the tar off many XY males. The US skier Lindsey Vonn, another XX female, can compete with the top fifteen men in world.

Sport also makes a lot of assumptions based on looks. If a woman looks the way she's "supposed to"—Vonn, who is blonde and beautiful, is a good example—no one ever questions her gender or measures her testosterone levels. Dumaresq, on the other hand, was visibly strong. She was six feet tall. Some people who looked at her saw a threat to the XX women in her sport.

The facts told a different story: Dumaresq was moving up quickly in Canada, but in international competitions, she wasn't a threat. She wasn't even competitive. At her peak, she was ranked only sixty-fourth. Many, many XX women were kicking her ass right, left and centre. Her being a transitioned athlete was giving her no advantage. She had a long way to go, but that was fine with her. Like me, she was in it for the "right" reasons: she loved sport, and wanted to play. The facts, however, didn't stop articles like the one published by the *National Post*, which reiterated the myth that because Dumaresq was "a man," she had "competitive advantages."

I wanted to support Dumaresq, but I was nervous—I wasn't yet competing as Kristen, I hadn't come out to anyone in the sport world, and I wasn't sure I was ready. After one too many people called Dumaresq "a guy," though, I'd had enough. I phoned Dr. Ross Outerbridge, an orthopaedic surgeon in Kamloops who had been the head of the World Water Skiing Medical Commission. He'd been very supportive to me when I was a junior skier, and I knew he'd keep my confidence.

He would be the first ranking person in sport who would find out about the new me. I didn't know how he'd respond. No matter how many people reassure you that you won't lose their friendship, sometimes who you are is too much for them to handle. I steeled myself and began, "I have been through an experience." To my relief, he was supportive.

"Are you watching what's happening to Michelle?" I then asked him. "I might be able to help." He offered to put me in contact with people he trusted—in Sport Canada, the Canadian Centre for Ethics in Sport (CCES, which is Canada's anti-doping body), the Canadian Association for the Advancement of Women in Sport (CAAWS), AthletesCAN, and Cycling Canada—so I could tell them what I'd learned about brain science, transitioning, and XY females.

I hung up the phone and exhaled shakily. This was a big deal. Everyone in sport would now find out about me. After my accident and during my transition, I wasn't riding competitively; I'd stepped away from the sport community. But I had a lot of relevant information. I felt it was my duty to step back in and help this young athlete.

The future of Dumaresq's career as a competitive cyclist was in the hands of two organizations: a Canadian body, Cycling Canada, which is based in Ottawa; and an international one, Union Cycliste Internationale (UCI), which is based in Aigle, Switzerland. A few days after I spoke to Outerbridge, those two organizations pulled Dumaresq's cycling licence, with the backing of the CCES. Their rationale seemed to be, "We don't have a procedure to deal with an athlete like this, so we'll eliminate the problem by taking her licence away."

Outerbridge and I began working the phones. Within two days, I received a flurry of responses. David McCrindle, the head of policy development for Sport Canada, called me from Hull. A delightful, smart man, McCrindle supported diversity and was trying to move it forward within his organization. His questions were all about how to help Dumaresq, and how to help sport. He admitted he knew little and wanted to learn. I also heard from Jennifer Birch-Jones, from CAAWS; Guy Tanguay, CEO of AthletesCAN; Joseph de Pencier, a lawyer for CCES; and *Cycling Canada* magazine. (Another tough decision. To come out via phone to a few trusted individuals was hard enough. But to come out to *Cycling Canada?* That scared me.)

I put together a quick but comprehensive primer of what it means to be a transitioned individual in sport, and emailed it to UCI. They reviewed it. Three weeks later, they quietly gave Dumaresq her licence back. She went on to compete for two more years, in Canada and internationally. I was delighted, but with one small reservation: I wish my Canadian government agencies had publicly acknowledged that they'd made a mistake, and corrected it. It might have made the road smoother for all who came after, including me.

Dumaresq contacted me to thank me. She was the first transitioned athlete I met (I didn't know that many transitioned people, period), so I expected to feel some sort of *aha* moment—someone like me! But that didn't happen. Because Dumaresq isn't like me. She's happy-go-lucky, a bit footloose and fancy-free. We became friendly, but having this one thing in common does not automatically guarantee friendship.

When I got involved with Dumaresq's case, I'd thought my goal was to correct the ignorance of what was happening to her. Afterward, I realized I might have a different goal: I might want to come back and compete as Kristen. What if sport could be something I passionately wanted to do, rather than just be an escape for Chris? Tentatively, I started to train.

At almost the same moment, October 2003, in advance of the 2004 Athens Olympics, the IOC convened an ad hoc committee in Stockholm to discuss participation of individuals who'd undergone sex reassignment—as they put it, "male to female and vice-versa." (In other words, we worry a lot about male to female, and not so much about the other one.) On the committee were Arne Ljungqvist, a professor from Sweden who served as the IOC's medical director; professor Odile Cohen-Haguenauer of France; professor Myron Genel (US); professor Joe Leigh Simpson (US); professor Martin Ritzén (Sweden); Marc Fellous (France); and Patrick Schamasch (France).

Not a single woman among them. Most of them didn't hold medical degrees—including Ljungqvist, the medical director. Yet they passed what's now known as the Stockholm Consensus. Transitioned athletes can compete, they said, if and only if they fit the IOC's definition.

That definition was, to put it mildly, ill-conceived. Without offering any supporting research, the committee "confirmed" that anyone changing male to female before puberty should be regarded as female, and vice versa. That's absurd. In Canada, as in many countries, a person is not allowed to transition, legally, before the age of eighteen. These administrators didn't know that basic fact.

As to sex reassignment after puberty, the committee decreed that male-to-female transitioned athletes would be eligible under the following conditions: "Surgical anatomical changes have been completed at least two years prior to the competition, including external genitalia changes and gonadectomy." That's awfully specific. Not everyone who transitions has such extensive surgery.

Another condition: "Legal recognition of their assigned sex has been acknowledged by their government." But many governments around the world do not acknowledge transitioned people, so this is a huge barrier for many athletes, which the IOC should not blithely overlook.

The panel also decreed that "hormonal therapy has been administered in a verifiable manner and for a sufficient length of time to minimize gender-related advantages in sport competitions." That's the key phrase: "gender-related advantages." Again, they assume anyone XY will always beat anyone XX.

The report continued that XY women who want to compete will be reviewed on "a confidential case-by-case basis." (If you recall the prologue, you'll understand that their definition of "confidential" was pretty loose.) And, "If questioned, the medical delegate *shall have the authority to take all appropriate measures* [italics mine] for the determination of the gender of the competitor." In other words, the IOC gives itself the authority to carry out invasive, humiliating gender verification procedures, on women only; no one ever asks male athletes to prove they're "real men."

The IOC's history of gender verification of women dates back to the Mexico City Olympics in 1968, where all female athletes were made to parade naked in front of officials. (Of course, that would verify only their biological sex, not their gender, but the IOC didn't make those distinctions.) At the 1976 Olympics in Montreal, the members of the East German women's swim team were born XX—they just took so many androgens that at least one of them transitioned. In 1992, the International Association of Athletics Foundations (IAAF) stopped screening every female athlete, but reserved the right to assess any participant about whom suspicions had arisen (usually, if one of her competitors complained). The IOC made a similar move in 1996.

The Stockholm Consensus updated the rules governing who was and was not permitted to compete. But—this is truly shocking—it wasn't based on any science. Why did an athlete have to be two years post-transition? They couldn't say.

As well, they decreed that the appropriate level for testosterone in XY females is 10 nanomoles per litre (NPL) in serum. (That's a tiny amount. A mole is a unit of measurement used in chemistry. It's what atomic weights are based on. One mole equals anything that contains this large number—six followed by twenty-three zeros—of molecules or atoms. A nanomole is one-billionth of a mole.)

The big question is, how did the Stockholm Consensus panel arrive at that figure? They've never answered that question, or provided any studies to back it up.

Well, I've studied this. Here's what I've learned.

XX women produce testosterone in their ovaries; XY men in their testicles. (I, of course, now have neither.) Testosterone is as vital to XX people as it is to XY people. It plays a role in nearly two hundred different daily body functions. People need testosterone to bring oxygen into their muscles, to regenerate red blood cells, and to build and repair muscle tissue. It acts as a communicator between cells and organs. If you remove it, the body loses its ability to communicate with itself, and some cells that are essential to basic metabolic function can no longer reproduce themselves. Without testosterone, people suffer a spectrum of maladies including chronic fatigue, diminished libido, depression, sleep disturbance, weight gain, loss of muscle mass, muscle aches, joint pain and lethargy.

But because testosterone is often a component in illegal performance-enhancing drug cocktails, the IOC, the World Anti-Doping Association, and the IAAF created strict policies around its use. It's a sad fact: some athletes do cheat. Some of that cheating is baked into the sports world. The Olympics is a spectacle—the more its athletes break records, the more coin the International Olympic Committee rakes in. Sport needs its athletes to go higher, faster and stronger year after year, to keep up its ratings. Without enhancements, that's hard to do. I'm not justifying said cheating. I certainly wouldn't do it. But I can understand it.

Here's an important distinction, though: sport organizations do not test the testosterone levels of XY male athletes. No male athlete has ever been accused of having a genetic advantage because he's "too manly." No one measures their testosterone to make sure they don't have "an unfair amount" or more than the next guy.

Nor do they limit the amount of testosterone that transitioned XX males can take. Chris Mosier, an XX male, is a good example. He's an inspirational figure: in 2015 he became the first transitioned athlete to qualify for a US national team (his sport is the duathlon), and the first to land a big endorsement contract. His Nike ad debuted during the Rio Olympics in 2016. The ad won awards, and positions Mosier as a trailblazer and a role model.

All that is great. But please note: WADA doesn't regulate Mosier's testosterone intake. Unlike XY females, the amount of testosterone he's allowed to take has no upper limit. Remember, XX bodies are built differently than XY bodies (see the "organizing effects" discussion, above.) A person born in an XX body needs testosterone, but doesn't make as much as a person born XY. So the testosterone receptors in XX bodies are much more sensitive—they do more with less. Therefore, whatever testosterone Mosier and other XX males take will go a lot further. They can hyper-perform. But the IOC and IAAF don't care about that, because XX males aren't perceived as a threat—how could anyone born in an XX body beat someone born XY?

According to sport, only women can have "too much" testosterone. Sport bodies apply these policies to all women athletes—to XY women like me; to XX women who were born, for whatever reasons, with higher than average testosterone levels; and to any women, regardless of genetic variation, who look "too masculine" for their taste. Sport enforces these policies rigorously.

The problem is, the IOC, IAAF and WADA plucked that "too much" number—10 NPL—out of thin air. The figure has no basis in science. There's no data behind it. It does not take into account the individual needs of our infinitely varied human brains. It's not focused on athlete health.

On average, healthy XX females have 1.5 to 3.5 NPL of testosterone. But (this bears repeating) in an XX body, the testosterone receptors are more sensitive; they use that amount more efficiently. The receptors in XY bodies, accustomed to having more testosterone, aren't as efficient. Although I'd transitioned, my testosterone receptors hadn't. Once my (or anyone's) brain's organizing effects are built, they can't be changed. So it stands to reason that, to be healthy, an XY female like me needs more testosterone—not as much as the average XY man, but more than the average XX woman.

As I've mentioned, this science is relatively new. There are no established norms on what an XY female's testosterone level should be, because not enough data have been collected. And because every brain is different, some will need more than others. For the IOC to pluck the number 10 NPL out of thin air, without any scientific backing, is irresponsible, harmful, and even potentially lethal.

There is also no proven correlation between testosterone and athletic performance. Some studies show that the hormone helps, but to what degree has not been determined. And even then, higher testosterone levels don't guarantee that you'll win; not even close. You have to have skills, talent, the discipline to train, and the will to compete. You couldn't take someone off the street, give them a super-sized dose of testosterone and expect that suddenly they'd excel at sports.

If the IOC trusted athletes, they would trust their endocrinologists and family doctors to set the appropriate level of testosterone for each individual competitor, instead of having a blanket, one-size-must-fit-all number. Yes, it would make things a little more complicated for them. But they already have a system for people with unique medical needs, called the therapeutic use exemption (TUE). All they'd have to do is broaden that policy.

Instead, they marginalize people like me, and discourage

or outright bar us from participating. They assume XY women are cheats, men in drag who want to beat women. They body-shame us, gender-test us, and strip us of our medals until they determine whether we are "woman enough" to earn them. To reiterate, they only do these things to XY women and to women who look "different."

Obviously I'm passionate about this, but it's an important discussion. Sport is often the gateway for change in society. The Paralympics, for example, helped broaden our perceptions of the differently abled by showcasing their amazing accomplishments. If the IOC, IAAF, WADA and the organizations that answer to them wanted to, they could make profound strides toward inclusivity, toward welcoming all people and all diversities into sport. (As I write this, the Commonwealth Games is doing that very thing.) However, for such a change of direction to be made, the people who run the IOC, IAAF and WADA—who are predominantly older, white, cisgendered, privileged men— would have to be willing to listen to people like me, to learn the science, and to amend their policies.

The sport world and society at large are conditioned to think that XX is the "only" woman and that XY is the "real" man. But science is moving us in a new direction. We are learning that gender and sexuality are fluid; brains and bodies are infinitely diverse. Humankind has had to radically revise our thinking many times in our evolution—we had to accept, for example, that the Earth revolves around the sun. This new thinking about gender, sexual orientation and the brain isn't as radical as that. But it will require a substantial societal shift. I believe sport can lead that shift. I believe it so strongly, I've staked my life on it.

The International Olympic Committee, however, doesn't agree. In a written addendum to the Stockholm Consensus, the IOC's medical director, Arne Ljungqvist, made his prejudices abundantly clear: "Although individuals who undergo sex reassignment usually have personal problems that make sports competition an unlikely activity for them, there are some for whom the participation in sport is possible." That is a sweeping presumption. He never produced any evidence for that, either.

That sentence troubled me so much that the minute I read it, I wrote Ljungqvist an email, and cc'd Sport Canada, other Canadian sport overseers and the IOC. It read, "I've competed for my country in two sports. I'm a design engineer. Can you tell me what personal problems I have that would take away my opportunity to participate?" I added, "It's people like you, who write things like this, that make my participation unlikely. It has nothing to do with me." He never replied, nor did anyone from the IOC. Nor did anyone from Canada.

Throughout my time working on this cause, people who

care about me have cautioned me against sending emails like the one above. They tell me I should soften my language, that I'm too confrontational. They tell me not to cc so many people, because it embarrasses the subjects and puts them on the spot. They say if I were more diplomatic I'd get further. Sometimes I listen to them. Mostly I don't. It's just not who I am.

As wrong-headed as the Stockholm Consensus was, it did open a door for me to compete, which I vowed to walk through. But first I had to get back on my bike.

In early 2005, the Forest City Velodrome opened in London, Ontario. It's one of only five indoor cycling tracks in all of North America. It's the shortest velodrome in the world, 138 metres, which means the track is steep and tight. The straights are 17 degrees, and the bankings (the corners) rise to 50 degrees. You have to maintain a consistent pedalling speed, at least 35 km/h, just to stay upright. And when you climb high into the corners and swing down, you can feel the G-forces pushing you into the track.

The bikes are fixed gear (single gear), no brakes. It's all about your leg speed—how fast you spin the pedals. On a road bike, you might do 80 to 95 revolutions per minute. On a track bike, it's 95 to 120 revs per minute.

It's cycling at its simplest level. It's a controlled environment. You always go counter-clockwise. The track never changes. There's little wind resistance. So success is about discipline, which I love. There's such a connection between you, your bike and the track, it's like you're one entity.

As Chris, I'd been a road racer, and I'd been out of the game for nearly a decade. Track racing gave me an opportunity for a fresh start: new name, new body, new sport.

The first time I drove to the track to train, I fretted for the entire two-hour trip from Toronto to London. Who would I run into? Despite my anxieties, I'd lived a life of white privilege. Now my diversity was plain to see, and I'd not yet developed self-protection techniques. Would people treat me cruelly? Would someone immediately out me, the way they'd outed Dumaresq?

Once in the velodrome, I recognized a few people, but I didn't say anything to them. I knew I'd be a curiosity: no one in sport had ever heard of Kristen Worley. At thirty-seven, I was pretty old for a newcomer. Yet it would be obvious that I'd been trained.

I got on my bike and started to ride, and my worries rushed away. All I could feel were the delicious demands of the endeavour. A minimum training session is five hundred laps in two hours, and my first session felt almost spiritual. I was connected to my body and my bike. I was riding as Kristen in a public space. On the bike paths of Toronto, no one really sees you as you whiz by. But a track is an auditorium. There are spectators, and they watch your entire lap, lap after lap.

After qualifying, I started to train there several times a week. It was a high. All the Pavlovian responses I'd developed to sport, the good feelings that whooshed up in me when I trained hard—even when I simply swung my leg over the saddle—returned. But I needed to figure out if I could be competitive in my new body. Everything had changed so significantly: how I sat on the saddle, how my bike was set up, my power-to-strength ratios.

I connected with a few other athletes, both men and women. I especially loved a group of riders in their seventies, from England and Ireland. After practice I'd join them in the upper corners of the bleachers and listen to their stories of racing in Europe. Soon I caught the eye of Rob Good, the coach of the Ontario and national track cycle teams. I told him my whole story, and he encouraged me to get my licence.

I'd had my surgery in 2004. Under the new Stockholm Consensus, I would be eligible to compete in 2006. Which meant I could shoot for the 2008 Olympics in Beijing. But to get my licence, I had to be gender-tested and verified as a woman by my own cycling association, in Ontario, as per the rules set out by the IOC. I agreed to go through their process.

As I detailed in the prologue, I was the first person anywhere in the world to be gender-tested under the new rule. The men who tested me had no idea what they were doing. The process they cooked up was barbaric, enraging and mortifying. They gave no thought to respecting my rights or protecting me as an athlete or a person. Afterward, I registered official complaints with all my federations: Cycling Ontario, CCES, Sport Canada, the Canadian Olympic Committee, and WADA. Sport Canada actually responded, by creating an ad-hoc group to deal with "transitioned athletes." But once again, that group included no transitioned athletes or genetic experts.

I didn't know what to do with my anger. I had nothing to compare my situation to, and no one to talk to. Sport was supposed to be my refuge, not my enemy. My country, Canada, was held up as a beacon of light to the oppressed. But its agencies were oppressing me. As always, Ali tried to help me through it, but she had only so much patience.

Then I read an article on the internet about Mianne Bagger, an Australian touring golfer, a transitioned XY female like me, and the first transitioned female to play professionally on the Australian and European tours. (Golf at that point had no association to the Olympics, so Mianne had been able to continue her career without the roadblocks thrown up by the IOC.) I sent her an email introducing myself. She wrote back in a day or two and we began corresponding—and continued to for fourteen years, sometimes every other day.

Mianne is articulate, a big thinker, focused on the greater good. For her, there's no such thing as a "diverse person"—every person is his or her own unique diversity.

We both resisted the LGBT label. First of all, L, G and B refer to sexuality, and T to gender; they're not the same issue, and they shouldn't be lumped together. Second, neither Mianne nor I like to be put in boxes. We'd fought our whole lives to break out of the boxes people put us into. So why define ourselves in terms that cram us into a different one?

Mianne encouraged me to pay attention to everything that was happening at the intersection of sport and gender, and to involve myself in it in any way I could be useful. Hmm, I thought. Why not start at the top?

One morning, I picked up the phone in my coach house and called the IOC in Lausanne. "I'd like to speak to Jacques Rogge, please," I said to the operator. I told her my name, and that I was a Canadian athlete.

This was nervy. Rogge, a Belgian, was the president of the IOC (from 2001 to 2013). He'd been an Olympic fin class sailor, a sports administrator and a physician. He was also a count. Everyone assumes guys like him are unreachable. Yet after a click, he was on the line.

He knew who I was: I was the first athlete to be gender-tested under the Stockholm Consensus, and I'd complained about the process publicly. "I've been meaning to talk to you," Rogge said. "This is a medical problem. I've been talking to Arne and Patrick"—Ljungqvist and Schamasch, who helped draft the Stockholm Consensus. "I put them in charge."

Very politely, I replied, "Dr. Rogge, you're wrong. This is not a medical problem. This is a social problem."

He let out a little grunt—"Aww, Kristen"—and said he'd be in touch.

Huh, I thought. That was easy. So I picked up the phone again, and redialed the IOC. The same operator answered. This time I asked for Patrick Schamasch, the IOC medical and scientific director (until 2012). "One moment, *madame*," the operator said. Another click, and Schamasch was on the line. He sounded out of breath.

"Kristen! I came out of a meeting to talk to you," he said. He, too, knew my story. I told him I'd just spoken to Rogge. He said that he didn't have time to talk right then. "But let's make some time next month."

I was on a roll. So I sat down and wrote an email to Chris Rudge, the CEO of the Canadian Olympic Committee (later the CEO of the Canadian Football League). Rudge was very good at assuring people that he was a leader in the realm of diversity in Canadian sport, but less good at doing anything about it. I told him that in the space of ten minutes, I had spoken to both Rogge and Schamasch. Both of them knew who I was, and said they'd been wanting to talk to me. Would Rudge talk to me? He didn't respond to my email.

The next day, May 6, I got a call from Michael Chambers,

the vice-president of the COC, from his law offices in Ottawa. It appears Rudge had alerted Chambers. Chambers implied that I had no business contacting Rogge or anyone else in Lausanne. "I never get to speak to Jacques or Patrick or Arne," he said. That really surprised me. Vancouver was soon to host the 2010 Games—why wasn't the COC able to speak directly to the heads of the IOC? And why was the COC okay with that?

A few weeks later, Schamasch suffered a heart attack. So the follow-up call he'd promised me was postponed until September. When the time finally came, I chose the participants, coordinated the time, and paid for the call myself, because I wanted to be in control. I also took detailed notes. On the line were: Schamasch; Mianne Bagger; Jameson Green, a transitioned XX male who is a well-known international academic and head of the World Professional Association for Transgender Health; David McCrindle, the manager of Sport Canada's Sport Participation Policy; Joseph de Pencier, the general legal counsel for the CCES; Tom Scrimger, director general of Sport Canada; and Chris Rudge from the Canadian Olympic Committee.

Just as the call began, Rudge ducked out. "I'm on a train," he said, "I can't be on the call." It was such a cop-out, I actually started laughing.

Mianne and I did most of the talking. I told everyone about my experience with their gender verification process. At first, Schamasch was pleasant. But about twenty minutes into the call, he began to snap at me. For instance, I asked him, "What research did you use to develop your policy?" A fair question, I thought.

He responded, "What do you mean? We had an expert panel."

Mianne and I explained, briefly, the science of what happens in our bodies. We said that the people conducting the verification didn't know enough about it. He said, "That's just the way it is."

I responded, "You're empowering people who know nothing of the science to violate athletes, and under the banner of the IOC."

He replied, "If you want to come to the Games, you play by my rules."

I said, "That's unethical. You can't do that to a human being."

He said, "I can do anything I want."

I can do anything I want. That was chilling. But in that moment I heard Graham Worley's voice in my head, telling me, "No one is above the law." So I echoed his words: "Dr. Schamasch, that's wrong. No one is above the law."

For the first time, de Pencier's voice came on the line. (A good lawyer always knows when to step in.) "Joseph here," he said. "Patrick, what can we do to fix this?"

Schamasch replied, "Get Kristen to get me the research."

So it was official. I knew more than the IOC. And instead of being embarrassed by that, they ordered me to fix it.

I met another important ally that September, when I went to Regina to attend a forum organized by AthletesCAN, the association of Canada's national team athletes (including the Olympic teams). Someone from the Canadian Centre for Ethics in Sport made an anti-doping presentation. I stood up and asked why it didn't address the issue of gender diversity. The presenter had no answer.

But in the far corner of the room, a woman rose and said, "I understand what Kristen is asking." After the panel ended, I crossed the room and found her—Dr. Janice Forsythe, a former 10,000-metre runner, now an associate professor at the University of Western Ontario's Institute of Olympic Studies. Later she became president of it. (Now she's head of indigenous studies—she's part Cree.)

On Sunday afternoon, Janice and I spent two hours hunkered down in old vinyl office chairs in the hotel basement, talking non-stop about diversity. Tall, slender and strong— in her body and her personality—Janice is thoughtful and articulate. But she also has a silly, fun side. When we got home, we struck up an email correspondence. As I got deeper into activism, she became a rock-solid support and a voice of reason for me. She always reminded me to think through all sides of an issue, not just my own.

Over the next few years, I kept rattling cages. In December 2006, I gave interviews in support of Santhi

Soundarajan. Soundarajan, a Tamil track-and-field athlete, had recently won a silver medal at in the women's
800 metres at the Asian Games. After her win, the International Association of Athletics Federations (IAAF) subjected her to a sex-verification test: an intensive evaluation
by a gynecologist, a geneticist, an endocrinologist, a psychologist and an internal medicine specialist. Their report
said she failed their test, and "does not possess the sexual
characteristics of a woman." Five days later, Lalit Bhanot,
a joint secretary of the Indian Olympic Association, a
branch of the IOC, phoned Soundarajan and stripped
her of her medal. Humiliated, Soundarajan returned to her
village and fell into a serious depression. Months later,
she tried to kill herself by ingesting a type of poison used
by veterinarians. A friend found her vomiting uncontrolla-
bly and brought her to a hospital. Horrifying.

In March 2007, CAAWS named me one of the top
sportswomen in Canada—the first female athlete who'd
been through transition to receive this honour. I celebrated
by writing an email to Dick Pound, a former Canadian
swimming champion who was the first president of WADA.
Lance Armstrong's story was dominating headlines, and
testosterone use was being conflated with doping. I wanted
to explain to Pound that different athletes have different
needs that require a nuanced approach to endocrinology.

Because Armstrong had had a gonadectomy (a testicle
was removed to combat his cancer), his body was no longer

producing testosterone. Yet he was still cycling competitively. His body temperature was still being regulated; his
muscles were recovering. I knew from my own experience that this is possible only with adequate testosterone.
I knew he must be getting it from somewhere. I wasn't
accusing him of doping. I was pointing out that he had a
therapeutic need.

I was so naive! Pound read my email as a challenge.
He thought I was saying, "Armstrong is doping, and
WADA is letting him." (Now, that may well have been
true—Armstrong was a golden goose for the IOC; they
didn't want to lose him. And WADA had always done the
IOC's bidding. But that's not what I was saying.)

Pound shot back an email that threatened legal action
against me, and copied it to the IOC and many Canadian
sports bodies. I suspect he knew that I was a troublemaker
who'd questioned the IOC's gender-testing policy. I believe
he wanted to shut me down.

But I don't scare easily. Remember the conference call in
2006, when Schamasch said, "I can do anything I want,"
and then asked me to send him some research? In July 2007,
when WADA was updating its code for transitioned and
intersex athletes, Jameson Green and I followed through on
that. We wrote up a concise one-pager, full of scientific fact,
and sent it to Joseph de Pencier, the CCES lawyer who'd
acted as peacemaker on the call. De Pencier sent it to WADA.
WADA ignored it.

But in October 2007, I got a call out of the blue from Anita DeFrantz, at that time the only female IOC member in the world. An Olympic rower, she'd joined the IOC in 1985, at the age of thirty-three, and was now chair of the Women's Sports Commission. She told me she'd been gender-tested, too. She agreed that the research behind the Stockholm Consensus was sorely lacking, and said she supported my making waves.

In April 2008, I made another wave. The National Collegiate Athletic Association (NCAA) was developing a gender policy for intercollegiate sport in the United States. These policies would affect people aged fourteen to twenty-two in high school and collegiate sport across the country. I noticed several potential problems in the discussions around this policy, and sent them an email that spelled them out. This time someone listened. The association delayed the release of the policy to do more research. Nearly two years later, the NCAA sent me the revised policy—even though we'd had no contact since my initial email—and asked me to read it over before it went out. Though the policy was still lacking in science, it was gratifying to at least be included in the process.

Also in 2008, I worked on a policy paper with AthletesCAN titled "Promising Practices," about gender inclusion in sport. In February 2009, it was published. It was the first government-funded initiative to recognize and address the flaws in international policies, including the IOC's. It was more about education than action, but it detailed the five-decade history of gender testing. It demonstrated to the Canadian and international sport communities that Canada had concerns about these issues. Moira Lassen, CEO of AthletesCAN, one of the key instigators in getting this paper going (her daughter is a Canadian weight lifter), flew to Toronto from Ottawa a few days before the paper was released. She took me to lunch in Chinatown to show it to me. "You should be proud," she said. "This happened because of you." I hoped it would get some wheels rolling.

I was also working with an organization called Play the Game, based in Copenhagen, whose goal is to promote freedom of expression in sport. I consulted with them as they formed the Coalition of Athletes for Inclusion in Sport (CAIS), whose particular focus was on people who'd been excluded from sport due to genetic difference.

I'm telling you all this to show you that I was trying to be a team player. I was raising uncomfortable truths, but I was doing so because I still believed in sport. I still believed that if I showed sport bodies the truth, they would make positive changes. I thought my persistence would win out. I was wrong.

CHAPTER SEVEN

Roadblocks

《 《 《 • 》 》 》

In June 2009, the World Tennis Association gender-tested Sarah Gronert. She was born with a genetic diversity (intersex), but she was only ranked 625th in the world. I emailed the president of the WTA to complain. "She has no competitive advantage," I said. "You did this because she was born intersex. You wanted to intimidate her, to make her go away." Sarah was "approved," but she never competed again. This is how sport can drum out anyone whose diversity frightens them.

The next such case got the whole world's attention. In August 2009, Caster Semenya, a middle-distance runner from South Africa, won gold in the women's 800 metres at the World Championships in Berlin. The

IAAF asked—*required* is a better word—her to take a gender verification test to determine whether she had a "rare medical condition" that gave her an "unfair genetic advantage."

"Unfair genetic advantage" is a ridiculous phrase. Imagine if someone told a seven-foot-four NBA player than his height gave him an unfair genetic advantage. Or told Michael Phelps he couldn't swim because his long arms and webbed toes gave him an unfair genetic advantage. Imagine a sprinter saying that he didn't want to race against Usain Bolt because Bolt has the unfair genetic advantage of being able to run faster.

Caster's so-called advantage was that she was born with an intersex trait that resulted in testosterone levels higher than the typical XX female. (Her gender-test results weren't officially published, but they were widely reported, a leak that violated her privacy.) I publicly commented, on Twitter and elsewhere, about how wrong all this was. The IAAF and IOC rules were in place to prevent doping—taking something above and beyond your natural, biology-given level. Caster wasn't doping. She was being vilified for who she was.

I submitted an op-ed defending Caster to the *World Sports Law Report*, a journal based in England that publishes case law and news stories to do with issues of sports law. The journal's editor, Andy Brown, not only published my piece, he reported further on what I said and published a news follow-up. Soon after that, Brown organized a conference in London, "Tackling Doping in Sport." The IAAF was one of the sponsors. During the closing-night thank-you dinner, one of the attendees from the IAAF—Brown can't recall his name—stood up and clinked his glass to get people's attention. In a sarcastic voice, he suggested everyone toast Brown, "the guy who's trying to ruin competitive sport." Meaning, Brown and I were threats to sport because we'd raised the issue of science. As Brown told me later, "When you're a journalist, and someone does that to you, you immediately think, 'I guess there really is something going on here.'"

Semenya, I'm happy to say, fought back against the IAAF regulations. She retained a legal team, Dewey & LeBoeuf (who acted pro bono), and they asked me to join as a consultant. On September 7, Wilfred Daniels, Semenya's coach with Athletics South Africa (ASA), apologized for failing to protect her from public scrutiny and shaming, and resigned. In November, South Africa's sports ministry issued a statement that Semenya had reached an agreement with the IAAF to keep her medal and award.

The IAAF had humiliated her and violated her privacy just because she looked too masculine for their tastes. A number of athletes, including the retired sprinter Michael Johnson, lambasted the IAAF. Prominent South African civic leaders, commentators, politicians and activists characterized the controversy as racist, sexist and an affront to

Semenya's human rights. Throughout, Semenya remained admirably strong. In an interview with the South African magazine *YOU*, she said, "God made me the way I am and I accept myself."

Two months later—one month ahead of the 2010 Vancouver Olympics—the IOC gathered their so-called experts in Miami to discuss how to handle future cases of gender ambiguity, to avoid PR disasters like Semenya's. "Sometimes you come across cases that are uncertain and ambiguous, and it changes from being a sports matter to a medical matter," Ljungqvist told the Associated Press. "The general recommendation is obvious—they should be treated as medical cases in compliance with up-to-date procedures. But we have to be more specific in telling the sports people what that actually means and what they should do." (Did you catch that inference? "We tell sport what to do.")

I knew this Miami summit was about PR and not science, because Dr. Robert McDonald, the medical director for the Vancouver Games, had called Patrick Schamasch and asked for a seat at the table. "Canada has a lot of information on gender science," McDonald said.

"Ah," Schamasch replied, "You've been talking to Kristen." Schamasch told McDonald he couldn't come. So much for being open to science.

Timed to coincide with the Miami summit—intended as a direct rebuke to it—another group I'd been consulting with, the Coalition of Athletes for Inclusion in Sport, issued a petition to challenge the IOC's gender policy. It read, in part, "The IOC's long history of persecuting women who do not fit the IOC's narrow definition of gender has a humiliating and extremely upsetting impact on these women and is a violation of their dignity. . . . We urge the IOC to commit to equitable and inclusive sport processes, that do not marginalize a person based on . . . any factor that is irrelevant to a person's actual (rather than assumed) ability to participate in sport. We request that the IOC work with and listen to international professionals in relevant fields of expertise." The IOC ignored us.

The Canadian Olympic Committee did not want gender testing at the Vancouver Games. But Arne Ljungqvist did. He approached four Vancouver hospitals to do it; they all turned him down. Finally a Catholic medical centre in downtown Vancouver agreed to do it. If you think the host country controls an Olympics, you're mistaken. It doesn't matter that Canada invested billions of dollars. The Games belong to the IOC.

During the first week of the Olympics, I talked to as many media outlets as I could, telling them that athletes were being gender-tested on Canadian soil. Dan Smith, who was then president of Sport Canada, replied to the challenges that I and other people made by saying, "The government of Canada will never tell the IOC how to change policy."

That was disheartening. My country will allow its athletes to be violated until someone else fixes it. But it was also a call to action.

Back in January 2006, when my cycling licence finally arrived, I immediately put it to use. My first track race was the Ontario track championships. I came in third. This is okay, I thought. Let's see where this goes.

Track racing is a winter sport. In the northern hemisphere, it begins in early September and continues until Good Friday, the traditional start of road season. I preferred track racing—track cyclists are more skilled than road cyclists, and I was leery of having another accident like the one that broke Chris's pelvis. But by the time spring arrived, I decided to race and train year-round, for both road and track.

Some people were supportive. Journalists were writing about me (including a long profile in *The Globe and Mail*). Many other people were shockingly cruel, however. Some coaches would turn away from me; they didn't like it that I'd been allowed to race. People would heckle me from the sidelines with gender-phobic insults, or get in my face while I did my bicycle maintenance check. Fathers and husbands of my competitors would loom over me, threaten me: "How dare you compete against my daughter/wife." It messed with my head. Sponsorship and funding were difficult.

Yet something was troubling me a lot more than any of the above. It was becoming clear to me that my health was not good. On a long ride a healthy athlete will lose water, and then start to burn fat. Normally I'd lose up to eight pounds on a 120-to-140-kilometre ride. But without enough testosterone, my body wasn't communicating with itself that way. I was riding five hundred kilometres a week, and I wasn't losing an ounce. My metabolism was slowing.

A healthy athlete goes through repeated cycles per workout: the muscles weaken, the brain sends a message to the sex organs to send testosterone, the muscles revive, and so on. But I had no sex organs, so that message wasn't being received. A healthy athlete also recovers a few hours after a ride. It would take me four days. And I couldn't build or repair muscle—not crazy muscles, just normal muscle tissue. My body temperature wouldn't regulate itself, either—it would go up and not come down. I couldn't possibly qualify for the Beijing Olympics feeling like this.

I was still married to Ali at this point. She could see I was suffering. She helped me find an endocrinologist, Dr. Jerald Bain, who agreed that, even though I'm an XY female, I needed testosterone for my health. Bain helped me to apply to the Canadian Centre for Ethics in Sport for a therapeutic use exemption.

A TUE is not uncommon. If you are diabetic, for example, you apply for a TUE for your insulin. But in women's sport, testosterone is a dirty word. People hear it and think "doping." It's not a science-based reaction, it's a knee-jerk one. In July 2006, I became the first transitioned athlete in the world to request a TUE for testosterone as a necessity for basic health.

I was naive enough to think that because I'd recently undergone the CCES's very thorough gender verification to get my cycling licence, they would be familiar with my case. They would know intimately why I needed the androgens, and would grant my legitimate request.

I was wrong. The centre made me authenticate my gender all over again. For a typical TUE application, CCES selects three local physicians to review the applicant's file. The athlete doesn't know who they are, and vice versa. But because of my unique circumstance—I had no androgens, period—everyone knew whose application it was. The panel repeatedly requested additional medical information, as well as information regarding my mental health, sexuality and reasons for transition. I gritted my teeth and gave them everything they asked for.

It usually takes two weeks for a TUE to be granted. Mine took three years.

I wrote numerous letters to the CCES during this time, asking them about the holdup. Once or twice, I phoned Doug MacQuarrie, the centre's COO, in tears. "You're bending over backward to WADA, being way more cautious than you should be," I told him. "You're keeping me out of my sport." My shot at the 2008 Olympics was gone. I also missed the 2009 Pan Am Games trials, the 2009 Ontario Provincial Championships, and the 2009 National Track Championships.

I was crushed—of course I was. But there was a silver lining. Because I wasn't able to compete while waiting for my TUE, I had a lot more time to spend with Graham as he was dying of cancer. During the five and a half months he spent in Princess Margaret Hospital, I visited him every day. Some days I took my dog, Bella, in with me. I sat beside Graham, held his hand, tried to help him walk. Same for the last three weeks of his life, which he spent in palliative care at Sunnybrook Hospital. I needed to be there for him when he was at his weakest, because he'd been there for me at my weakest. It also inspired me to fight for what mattered to me. Graham died on June 6, 2008. D-Day.

At 6:30 p.m. on September 4, 2009, my phone rang. It was Anne Brown, the director general of the Canadian Centre for Ethics in Sport. In a teary voice, she announced, "You've been approved!" Forty milligrams of testosterone, once daily, oral. It was official. I was the first XY female athlete to receive a TUE for testosterone to maintain my health.

That was good news. But it was also frustrating. Brown's tears didn't mean, "This is something you need and deserve." Her tears meant, "We pulled off this big favour for you." I'd lost years of competition waiting for it. The approved androgen level was still extremely low for my XY body. The TUE was only good for one year; after that, I'd have to reapply. By contrast, XX males are often granted ten-year TUEs. As well, I had to have my blood tested every other month. Most TUE recipients are tested once, at most twice, per year.

Desperate to dive back into racing, I did everything they asked. And it did make me feel better in my daily life. Before my TUE, it was as if everything in my body had turned off. After, my brain started firing properly again. I'd gotten so used to feeling low; now I felt, "Ohhh, this is what normal feels like." It was like replacing a twenty-watt lightbulb with a one hundred-watt one.

For racing, however, it became clear within six months that the TUE-approved dosage wasn't enough for me. My blood tests showed that only a fraction of my daily oral dose was making it to my bloodstream. I needed to know how CCES and/or WADA had determined that dose. I'd never seen any science, from either of them.

I picked up the phone and called Oliver Rubin, WADA's chief scientist, in Montreal. He suggested that I contact WADA's athlete information line, a 1-800 number and an email address that all athletes have access to, supposedly designed for open communication about athlete and drug issues. So I carefully crafted an email. I said I'd been in touch with Dr. Rubin. I said I was greatly concerned with my health issues, and those of my fellow athletes. I asked, "As the world leaders in anti-doping, could WADA please share the science behind their decision?"

Three weeks later, in May 2011, I received a two-page cease-and-desist letter from the Montreal law firm representing John Fahey, the CEO of WADA, threatening to sue me if I persisted in this manner. Instead of answering my questions, they were trying to scare me so I'd stop asking.

Interestingly, that same month, the CCES invited me to participate in a two-day session at the National Arts Centre in Ottawa, to talk about gender policy in Canadian sport. Other participants included Bruce Kidd, an academic, author, former Olympian (in track and field) and honorary member of the Canadian Olympic Committee; Paul Melia, the CEO of CCES; John Dalla Costa, an international ethics expert and the founder of the Centre for Ethical Orientation; and medical professionals from across the country.

I'd guess our two days in Ottawa cost taxpayers at least $250,000—the Ministry of Sport flew us in, put us up in nice hotels, fed and fêted us with drinks. But of the sixteen of us at the table, perhaps two or three were experts in gender or endocrinology—and I'm including myself among them. Paul Melia didn't even know what the word "intersex" meant, and couldn't bring himself to say it for the entire first day. Others kept using words like "allow"—as in, we should allow these people to play—that signify mere tolerance, not real inclusion. I spoke on and off about my experience, and was frank about my disappointment with the way Canada was handling these issues—I said our system is based on sham science from Europe, and puts Canadians at risk.

Despite all that, I could tell that Dalla Costa, who moderated our discussions, had the right intentions. He wanted to write a useful paper about transgender, transitioned and intersex athletes, and include them in Canadian sport. He came up with a title, "Sport in Transition," that I loved, because for once it put the onus of change on sport, instead of on people to change their bodies to fit an ideology. I worked with him for the next ten months, emailing suggestions back and forth.

I remember the day I finally had to admit that my TUE dose wasn't working: June 25, 2011. I was racing in the Canadian road cycling championships, in Brampton. I was doing the criterium: a race in which riders do a specified number of laps, say sixty or one hundred, on a closed city-road circuit, a loop one or two kilometres long. It's exciting, fast and technical, with spectators on bleachers all around the course.

Halfway through the race, my body shut down. My temperature was stuck on high, my muscles stopped recovering.

It wasn't just emotionally draining, it was also physically painful. I had to take a DNF (did not finish). I was in tears.

I went to my car and called my cousin Michael McKee, an orthopedic surgeon, for a recommendation. He put me in touch with Dr. Anthony Galea, a world-renowned sports medicine expert—he'd been the supervising physician for numerous international sporting events, and had been the team physician for the Toronto Argonauts.

Galea was also a controversial figure. He was an early proponent of platelet-rich plasma therapy (PRP), which is supposed to speed soft-tissue repair. (You draw a patient's blood, spin it in a centrifuge to separate the platelets, and then inject the concentrated platelets into the injury site.) A Who's Who of sports stars, including the golfer Tiger Woods, the baseball slugger Alex Rodriguez, the Olympic runner Donovan Bailey and the figure skater Patrick Chan, came to Galea for PRP, and he travelled to them.

But not everyone understood PRP. In 2009, Galea had been arrested for smuggling human growth hormone into the United States. In 2011, he pleaded guilty to a lesser charge of bringing in mislabelled drugs, and was sentenced to one year of unsupervised release. However, athletes from around the world were still lining up to see him, which normally takes a year. Mike got me in in a week.

After numerous blood tests, Galea determined that I was testosterone-deficient, even for a woman. The small dose of testosterone I was allowed under my TUE wasn't enough. My red-blood cell count was extremely low—those cells can't regenerate without testosterone. My muscles were atrophying. Scientifically, I was suffocating on the bike. But if I increased my testosterone to a healthy level, I couldn't compete. Your health or your sport. No one should have to make that choice, but I chose health.

For months, Dr. Galea and I tried to find my ideal level: the lowest possible dose that would still allow me to compete, somewhere between the menopausal female and low-testosterone-male levels. He knew what dose he would give to an XY male. But he didn't want to give me anywhere near that amount because I also take estrogen, and he didn't want them fighting each other.

I was a human science project. Galea would settle on a dose and then watch me for three or four months, to see how I reacted to it. A normal male dose would be .5 to 1 milligram every two to three weeks. We started by injecting around .1 of a mill into my bum every three to four weeks. (I would have preferred a topical cream—it's easier and less painful—but money was always an issue, and injections are a lot cheaper.)

For a few days after a shot, I'd be able to train. But long before my next injection, I'd be too fatigued to get off my couch, much less onto my bike. So he'd up the dose a tiny amount. Then he'd watch for another three to four months. I kept a journal detailing how I felt physically and emotionally, and he would ask me questions:

Had any symptoms improved? Which ones? How had they improved? Was that adequate?

During this trial period I stepped away from competing in sanctioned races, but I still trained alongside the Ontario and national teams and coaches. As a racer, you get a little red pickup, a sensor device, which you attach to the front fork of your bike. It sends your lap and race times to a computer database. Over the months with Dr. Galea, as the dose inched up, you could see my times accelerate.

I didn't need a computer to tell me that I was doing better. I could feel it in every cell. During a race, even a training race, the pace is intense. You have to pedal constantly; there's no coasting or resting. And when there's a jump—when one rider accelerates suddenly—all the riders have to keep up or they're gone. With my TUE dose alone, I couldn't keep up. Now I could. I lost twenty pounds—my body could metabolize again. My times and speeds went up to levels equal with the best racers in Canada, who are among the best in the world. The Canadian coach, Rob Good, thought I had a shot at making the B pursuit track cycling team at the 2012 London Olympics.

To do that, I'd need a new TUE. I applied on March 12, 2012. Again, the process dragged on. I kept hoping for the best: I registered for the Women's Elite Road Cycling Nationals, to be held in Quebec on June 22. I even travelled there, hoping my TUE would be granted just in time. But it wasn't.

I was furious, and not just for myself. I was seeing road-blocks and misinformation everywhere. In May 2012, *Sports Illustrated* ran a big piece by Pablo Torre, pegged to the London Olympics, entitled "The Transgender Athlete." It was full of wrongheaded assumptions and flat-out errors. "Testosterone, which surges during male puberty," Torre wrote, "is the engine powering an array of a man's compet-itive advantages: greater height and weight, higher bone density, increased muscle mass and a greater proportion of oxygen-carrying red cells in the blood. Contrast this with estrogen's effects (accumulated fat on widened hips), and it is sensible enough to segregate athletes by sex. But the existence of openly transgender athletes compli-cates the question of who belongs where."

As soon as I finished the piece, I called him. I tried to tell him that this is how misinformation spreads—a story pulls so-called research off the internet, other stories quote that story, and on it goes. Society's presuppositions are reinforced, and those in power don't have to change. He listened, but didn't run a follow-up article.

In June 2012, Randall Garrison, an NDP MP from British Columbia, contacted me from the House of Commons. He was the sponsor of Bill C-279, whose pur-pose was to amend the Canadian Human Rights Act to prevent discrimination specifically based on gender identity. The bill had just gone to its first floor vote. Bal Gosal, a conservative MP from Bramalea who was the minister of sport under Stephen Harper, had voted against it.

I sat down and wrote an email to Minister Gosal, cc'ing a few other people, including Paul Melia and Doug MacQuarrie, the CEO and COO, respectively, of CCES. The "Sport in Transition" paper that Minister Gosal's ministry was funding was about to come out. At that point I'd been working on it for nearly a year. I wrote that if Minister Gosal was going to vote against the rights of gender-variant Canadians, I didn't want my name on anything that came from his ministry. With a heavy heart, I told him to remove my name from the document.

Melia called me, sounding curt. He knew the document was less authoritative without my name on it. But I didn't want people to read my name and think that I was on board with a government that didn't support gender rights. People join committees or draft papers for all kinds of political reasons, but there are real human beings at the end of those actions and real implications for them. When "Sport in Transition" was published in July 2012, some people who read it thought Canada was on the verge of significant change. But I knew we weren't. It just felt like one more way I'd failed.

In November 2012, another depressing thing happened with Bill C-279. Sport Canada had proposed a two-paragraph clause, which Garrison (the bill's author) sent to me. In part, it read, "No provision of the Act shall be construed so as to abrogate from the authority of the Minister of State for Sport, the Department of Canadian Heritage, Sport Canada or any governing body of Sport Canada to establish eligibility criteria for competing in events under its jurisdiction."

Garrison asked me, "What does this mean?"

I told him what it meant: that our Canadian sport bodies wanted to be excused from the Canadian Charter of Rights so they could continue to enforce their own "eligibility criteria." They cared more about conforming to IOC policy than to Canadian law. That was upsetting. (As was the death of the bill; it guttered out in February 2017.)

In December 2012, I set up a conference call with Sport Canada and CCES, to try to explain how their TUE and gender verification policies had failed me, and why they were wrong. On the call were Martin Boileau, the director general of Sport Canada; Rosemary Pitfield, CCES communications director; and John Dalla Costa, CCES's ethicist. Also on the call, to my surprise—I didn't invite them—were Dan Smith, the president of Sport Canada; and Dave McCrindle, Sport Canada's head of policy development.

Dalla Costa was on my side; together we tried to explain how Canada's gender verification and TUE policies were misguided. Boileau promised to talk to Greg Mathieu, the CEO of Cycling Canada, and get back to me.

I was the one who got back to him, sending him a reminder email. Boileau replied that he had spoken to Mathieu, and neither Sport Canada nor Cycling Canada would take any action. He shut me down in four sentences.

Then, and most important, on June 23, 2013, a physician in the United Kingdom leaked a harrowing story. Just before the London 2012 Olympics, four young women from South Asia, aged eighteen to twenty-one, were told they had to have surgery if they wanted to compete. They were intersex women with a condition called 5-alpha-reductase deficiency: they had undescended testicles, higher than average testosterone levels, and atypically large clitorises. Though they weren't medal winners, or even high-end performers, the IOC recommended to their local sport bodies that if they wanted to compete, they should have surgery to remove their gonads, which would lower their (natural) testosterone levels. And while they were at it, they should also have "feminine remodeling surgery" to reshape their genitals. The women didn't want or need these surgeries. They were castrated in the name of sport.

Andy Brown investigated this story for the *World Sports Law Report*. When he contacted the IAAF, they denied the surgeries had taken place. He dug up a 2013 study verifying that they had happened, and sent the IAAF follow-up emails. (The study doesn't specify names or home countries; Brown is still trying to contact the women.) As of this writing, the IAAF has yet to respond.

Other physicians reacted with horror—but not the horror you might expect. Dr. Gedis Grudzinskas, a leading gynecologist at London Bridge Hospital, said this case was "proof" that the IAAF and IOC should ban intersex women from competition altogether, or else risk "opening the door to abuse." He suggested that the surgery these young women endured might inspire "other men" to "neuter themselves" so they could compete against women. I read that, and I didn't know whether to weep or scream.

I emailed Ljungkvist at the IOC and asked if the young women were still in sport. He never replied. I also wrote to Charles Sultan from Montpellier University, who performed the surgery on the athletes. I told him he had no idea of the harm he'd done. He robbed them of their sexuality, their sexual identity, their mental health. Thankfully, I wasn't the only one to tell him these things. I don't know if it was a result of public pressure, but he ended up dissolving his medical practice. But it was too late for those young athletes.

People tell me not to take this stuff personally, but I don't listen. It is personal. Those of us with gender diversity are mistreated throughout our lives. When a publication like *Sports Illustrated*, a clause like the one proposed for Bill C-279, or a global behemoth like the IOC sanctions that mistreatment, the injustice sometimes overwhelms me.

Despite all that, I still hoped I could find a way to regain my health *and* race legally. In 2013, I again applied for my OCA membership and UCI race licence, but this time I asked to be exempted from the section of the UCI Race License Declaration that concerns their anti-doping and gender policies, on the grounds that they were discriminatory and adversely impacting my health. After consulting with Cycling Canada, the OCA denied my application. A representative from Canadian Cycling sent me this email: ". . . You want to enter into the competition system that is governed by the rules of the IOC and UCI, rules which we are required to uphold. . . . If you can't agree to the rules then you need to look for another competition system."

In November 2013, I contacted UCI and asked for the science behind its policies for XY females. Christian Varin, UCI Legal Services, replied that UCI followed the IOC's policies, and since their "recommendations are still in force, the UCI sees no reason to apply another policy."

In 2014, I again requested an exemption from UCI's anti-doping policies, and got the same answer. I was denied.

The sport world I loved was making me feel like a non-person, a liar who was trying to cheat. Dr. Galea had brought me back to health, and I was grateful for that. But why couldn't I have both health and sport? Why wasn't the system designed to help me? Why did the process have to be so difficult, unpleasant and demoralizing? Was it set up that way deliberately, so diverse people will just throw up our hands and say, "Screw this, I'm out"?

Maybe. Except I refused to say that.

CHAPTER EIGHT

The Lawsuit Begins

《 《 《 • 》 》 》

I'll give the IOC credit for one thing: it created a clever system to protect itself.

The licence that every elite athlete must sign to compete in any sport in any country binds that athlete to take all disputes to the Court of Arbitration for Sport (CAS) in Lausanne. That court is funded by—you guessed it—the IOC. It employs lawyers that also argue for the IOC. And it doesn't publish all its judgments. Andy Brown's research suggests that it tends to publish the judgments that go the IOC's way, but not the ones that don't. So a lawyer who is representing an athlete who is taking an argument to the court often cannot access the precedents needed to defend a client. Obviously, that gives sport organizations an inherent advantage over any challengers.

To give you an example of how byzantine things get at the court, I'll skip ahead a few years, to one of the more famous cases about gender and sport, involving the Indian sprinter Dutee Chand. Chand streaked onto the sports scene in 2012, becoming a national champion in the 100-metre dash. She went on to win more 100- and 200-metre races. But in 2014, the Athletic Federation of India stated that she was ineligible to compete at the Commonwealth Games due to her hyperandrogenism.

Hyperandrogenism is a genetic condition in which women have higher than typical testosterone levels. Chand's levels weren't unnaturally elevated; she was born that way. But her levels were higher than 10 NMOL (10 nanomoles per litre of blood), which the IOC and IAAF regulations call a "perceived advantage." The Indian federation was complying with their rules and the Olympic Charter.

"Perceived advantage"—that phrase again. I said this earlier but it bears repeating. One, no scientific evidence demonstrates a link between enhanced androgen levels and improved athletic performance. Two, this rule only applies to women—there is no regulation limiting the levels of testosterone in an XY or XX man. And three, one could argue that all elite athletes have some kind of genetic advantage—that's how they got to be elite athletes.

But India booted Chand off their Commonwealth Games teams. (And, not incidentally, violated her privacy by blaring her genetic diversity to the world.) She wanted to fight back. But because she had signed her sport licence, she had to bring her case to the Court of Arbitration in Sport. In 2015, the court announced its ruling: it did not strike down the no-science limit of 10 NMOL, but it gave the IAAF two years to find and file some scientific evidence in support of it.

When that deadline came and went, in July 2017, the court extended it by another two months. Then in January 2018, CAS postponed Chand's case for six more months and asked the IAAF to clarify whether it would replace the disputed regulations with new ones. If the IAAF modified its rules, the court would dismiss Chand's case. Pause here for a minute and digest that: CAS was giving the IAAF an out, and begging them to take it.

Pretty dizzying, right? Stick with me. The IAAF did modify its rules. In April 2018, it submitted new testosterone regulations to CAS, but these new regulations covered only certain events. Interestingly, Chand's events, the 100- and 200-metre races, weren't included. The events that were—the 400-, 800- and 1500-metre races—are the specialty of . . . Caster Semenya.

Semenya, the most dominant women's 800-metre runner of the last decade, wins more international races than Chand. These new regulations were a bald attempt to neuter her—to force her to choose between retirement and invasive treatment to reduce her natural testosterone.

"Lowering testosterone levels is not a benign intervention," Katrina Karkazis, a bioethicist at Yale University and the author of an upcoming book on testosterone, told the *Toronto Star* in April 2018. She warned of potential "short-term and long-term harm," and added, "If you radically lower anyone's testosterone, they will feel a very significant effect . . . No one lowers testosterone just because it's high. It's not cholesterol."

As of this writing, the IAAF hopes to implement its new rules in November 2018. But neither they nor the IOC have produced any scientific backing for the testosterone limits. (It's worth noting that even with her naturally higher testosterone level, Semenya's race times are still way off XY male times.) Meanwhile, the IAAF stole valuable race time from Chand, tarred her good name—and then avoided any consequence by ducking through the loophole CAS gave them. Her case was dropped, not ruled on, so she never had her grievance addressed.

Despite my reservations about the Court of Arbitration in Sport, I wanted to exhaust all the possibilities open to me. So back in March 2011, around the time I was applying for my second TUE, I spoke to an in-house counsel at the court. The lawyer had heard of me. "We knew this day would come, Kristen," he said. Then he promptly shooed me away. He said the court wasn't the appropriate body to address my particular concerns. It was set up for contract and anti-doping conflicts, not for medical issues.

As I've said, the three years from 2011 to 2014 were a dark period for me. Ali left me. I was stonewalled on repeated applications for a TUE. The London Olympics, my last chance to compete at that level, came and went. My dog, Bella, died. I felt all the ways a person can feel bad. I was angry. I wallowed in self-pity. I was frightened. I withdrew.

By September 2014, Ali and I were building a tentative friendship, and I'd adopted a new dog, a sweet-natured golden Lab named Arya. But I was lonely. I was feeling heartsick about the world. I missed the solace of sport. Then one morning, while I was working at my computer, I turned on the radio.

On the CBC, an Ontario human rights lawyer named Brenda Culbert was talking about a case she'd just concluded with the Ontario Human Rights Tribunal, challenging Hockey Canada on accessibility rights for transgender minor hockey players. The settlement they'd reached, which applied to all minor players in Ontario under the auspices of Hockey Canada, was terrific: The players would now be able to choose their dressing rooms and be addressed by their preferred names and pronouns. The policy also called for Hockey Canada to educate its trainers and coaches on discrimination, harassment, and gender identity and expression.

Listening to Culbert reminded me of what I loved about sport. Because so many people play sports, or watch them, sport is often at the vanguard of sweeping societal change. The tennis star Billie Jean King championed women's rights and furthered acceptance of lesbians in mainstream culture. Running blades created for elite athletes became widespread, and helped advance the rights of the differently abled. NFL players who took a knee sparked a conversation about institutionalized racism. Young people who play alongside diverse teammates learn not to fear or discriminate against diverse adults. Sport can be a force for good.

I'd been angry, but this victory felt like hope. It made me think maybe I could change something, too. Still, the thought of taking on Big Sport made me as nauseated as any lack of hormones ever had. If I was David, the IOC was Goliath times ten. But as I listened to Culbert, a lightbulb turned on above my head. My issue wasn't a sports issue. It was a human rights issue.

If the offices of the Human Rights Legal Support Centre in downtown Toronto were in a movie, the set description would read, "Utterly minimalist and unassuming. White walls, industrial overhead lights, a few metal chairs, a stand of pamphlets. The physical embodiment of generic." But don't be misled by its looks. It's a stealth lair for superheroes.

The centre advocates for Ontarians who've experienced discrimination contrary to Ontario's Human Rights Code. Its lawyers represent clients at mediations and hearings, and sometimes file applications at the Human Rights Tribunal of Ontario. Cases can impact groups, like the hockey case I mentioned above, or individuals; sometimes cash awards are paid out, sometimes not. One recent client was awarded $10,000 after being racially profiled by a restaurant; a fifteen-year-old female tattoo parlour worker won $75,000 from the employer who sexually harassed her.

But because it has to spend its government funds wisely, the centre does a lot of due diligence before it takes on a client. My initial call to Culbert lasted forty-five minutes. At first she suggested I take my case to GLAAD or You Can Play, organizations dedicated to the eradication of trans- and homophobia. I tried to explain that my issue shouldn't be pigeonholed as LGBTQ—it's about all human diversity. For a month, we talked and emailed back and forth, educating each other. Then she presented my case to her colleagues, and asked them whether the centre should take it on.

That was a nail-biter for me. If Culbert's partners didn't see this as a human rights issue, no one would. For her part, Culbert knew that the scope of the case was wider and more international than the Human Rights Tribunal of Ontario usually heard. It was one thing to challenge my provincial sport bodies. But proving that the IOC, an international organization based in Lausanne, had to answer to Ontario's Human Rights Code, would require skillful arguments.

When Brenda phoned me to say that the centre was on board, she took care to explain their reasons, but I was so excited, I could hardly take it in. Patiently, she repeated it until I was able to understand.

Reason one: they felt it was an important emerging issue. The IOC was sticking to a rigid binary position— male vs. female athletes, dopers vs. non-dopers—while other sport organizations, such as the Commonwealth Games, and society in general, were moving toward more fluid gender concepts. The IOC and WADA certainly weren't out there leading the way; in fact, they'd resisted turning their minds to the subtleties and intricacies of the issue.

Reason two: the centre likes to take cases that will move the law. That's part of its mandate.

Reason three: Culbert said, was my commitment and passion. She told me she'd never had as intense a relationship with a client as she had with me. She let me contact her at all hours. She let me all the way in.

Gulp. We were off.

For the next year, Culbert and I met and talked

regularly. I sent her a mountain of emails—updated medical information, studies on the impact of testosterone on performance, profiles of other athletes, articles about the history of gender testing. She had no idea that XY females were treated with estrogen, but were deprived of testosterone. The health impact of that really struck her—she thought it was important to let the wider world know that people who tried to follow WADA's guidelines could really hurt themselves.

Together, we formulated the language we would use. The sport organizations used terms like "disorders of sex development" and "gender disorders." Those terms suggest maladies, things that need to be corrected. We agreed it was important that we say, instead, "variations of sex development" and "gender variations"—things that occur naturally, whether or not they're later modified by surgery. (It's amazing to see how language itself can create biases, isn't it?)

I wanted us to pay special attention to the gender terminology. The general public was still using derogatory terms like "tranny" and "he/she," and even well-intentioned people were stuck on making distinctions: Was I transgendered, or had I transitioned? I needed Culbert to understand that my personal genitalia wasn't the point, and that those words were a mask that kept people from seeing the discrimination underneath them: they were code words for "less female," "less of a woman." *Less than.*

If we stick to XY woman and XX woman, XY man and XX man, I argued, not only is that clearer to everyone, it also makes all genders *equal to*. And it keeps the argument out of my underpants.

This was also vitally important to me: I didn't want us to argue that I deserved to compete because I had medically transitioned, and therefore had "solved my problem." I wanted us to argue that I deserved to compete because I was a human being.

At the same time, Culbert and her team were sharpening their legal focus. My story involved a lot of actors and a lot of moving parts, and they had to learn fast to put it all together. With me, they had a real case. The question was, how many organizations could they draw into it? They had to figure out how the Ontario Human Rights Tribunal fit in, because the tribunal has a limited statutory jurisdiction. It doesn't solve all problems or all unfairness. It deals with specific kinds of discrimination in Ontario.

The centre certainly could make the argument that the Ontario Cycling Association, the group that physically issued my licence, had violated my human rights via their intrusive gender verification and TUE policies. And it wasn't much of a stretch to say that Cycling Canada, the national organization, bore prior responsibility for that, because Ontario follows policies set out by Canada.

But Canadian athletes also want to compete internationally, and in the Olympics. In order for them to do that, they must follow the rules of international organizations—in my case, Union Cycliste Internationale. And the rules those organizations follow are set by the IOC.

So that was our argument. We would demonstrate a direct causal relationship: The IOC had made a policy that was unsupported by science and violated human rights. It enacted that policy upon all of the citizens of the 205 nations in the Olympic movement, and upon all the organizations under its umbrella, such as UCI. UCI then imposed those IOC policies on Cycling Canada, Cycling Canada imposed them on the Ontario Cycling Association, and the provincial association imposed them on me. To put it another way, they violated my human rights because the IOC told them they had to.

This seemed super-clear to me, and so exciting. Culbert felt she had to caution me: there is what we perceive to be logical and correct and obvious, and then there is the law. They don't always agree. She also cautioned me that my personal credibility likely would be attacked.

I didn't care. I'd had enough of sport telling me who I wasn't. I was ready to show them who I was.

In early May 2015, Brenda and I filed our first application to the Human Rights Tribunal of Ontario. They came back with a request: give the Ontario Cycling Association one final chance to respond.

On May 7, I sent the OCA an email from my account, blind-copying Brenda. I stated my argument one more time: I needed my hormones, not for doping, but for my basic health. I couldn't get a TUE. Subjecting me to further gender verification was a violation of my human rights. But I still wanted a race licence. Given those conditions, could I be exempted on medical grounds from the anti-doping declaration in the UCI Race Licence application? We gave the OCA a month to respond. It never even replied. (Later, the association told me that it never received the email—but if it had, it would have denied my request. Sigh.)

On June 30, 2015, the Human Rights Legal Support Centre and I held hands and jumped: we filed an action against the Ontario Cycling Association, Cycling Canada, Union Cycliste Internationale, and the International Olympic Committee to the Human Rights Tribunal of Ontario, charging those organizations with human rights violations. (In November 2015, we added WADA to that list.)

It gets detailed here, so please bear with me. You need to know that the tribunal is a statutory, administrative, decision-making body that applies the human rights code of Ontario; it is not exactly a "court." It holds hearings, not trials. After I filed my application (a statement of claim) with the tribunal, the IOC, UCI and, later, WADA filed their response: they brought a preliminary motion to get my application dismissed even before a hearing was held on its merits—before any evidence was heard. The Ontario tribunal, they said, did not have jurisdiction over them. They also questioned whether I had "a reasonable prospect of success" in establishing that discrimination had occurred. My team expected that. We made a reply to those issues—seventy-nine pages of detailed rebuttal on every point. The tribunal said they'd hear our arguments in April 2016.

The IOC also brought a second application, called a judicial review application, before the Ontario Superior Court of Justice—what we think of as proper court. The IOC wanted the Superior Court to say that the tribunal should not even be allowed to decide if it had jurisdiction, because in their opinion, it was clear they didn't. The IOC was playing hardball, but again, that's not unusual. A separate date was set for that: February 29, 2016.

Toby Young, Culbert's boss at the centre, asked the IOC numerous times to reconsider this February court appearance. His position was that the IOC should go before the tribunal in April along with the other organizations named in our action, and hear whether the tribunal thought it had jurisdiction or not. If the tribunal agreed that it didn't—which could well happen—the IOC won. If the tribunal said it did have jurisdiction, *then* the IOC could go to Superior Court to argue that it didn't.

The IOC, however, dug in its heels: it didn't agree that the tribunal had the authority to claim jurisdiction in this context. It refused to participate. And it wanted the Superior Court to tell us so.

Then, in January 2016, the IOC's medical officials published new policy guidelines—perhaps as a response to my suit, perhaps not. "Transgendered people should be allowed to compete without undergoing sex reassignment surgery," these guidelines said. To be clear, that wasn't my argument with them; I wanted to address testosterone levels, TUEs and gender verification. But it was an interesting deflection.

This new policy was created to update the Stockholm Consensus of 2003, which, as you may recall, did require gender diverse athletes to have surgery, followed by two years of hormone therapy. Now, surgery would no longer be required. Female-to-male transitioned athletes (XX males) would be eligible to take part in men's competitions "without restriction." Male-to-female transitioned athletes (XY females) would need to demonstrate—wait for it—that their testosterone level was below 10 NPL for one year before competing: 10 NPL, our old, still-unscientifically-proven friend.

Our other old friend, Arne Ljungqvist, who co-wrote the new policy, told the Associated Press that the new consensus was driven by social and political changes. "It has become much more of a social issue than in the past," he said. "We had to review and look into this from a new angle. We needed to adapt to the modern legislation around the world. We felt we cannot impose a surgery if that is no longer a legal requirement.

"Those cases are very few, but we had to answer the question," he continued. "It is an adaptation to a human rights issue. This is an important matter. It's a trend of being more flexible and more liberal."

So why were the IOC's policies toward XY females and XX males still different? The same old song: "The overriding objective is and remains the guarantee of fair competition," the new policy read. They still believed that XY females had an "unfair advantage."

As a further reminder that the IOC was not actually being "more liberal and flexible," Ljungqvist added, "If you change sex, you will have to have a hormone level below 10 NPL for twelve months. That does not mean a one-year guarantee. You don't go below 10 from day one. It takes quite some time. It can take more than one year or two years." In other words, the IOC could still keep intersex and XY females out of sport for as long as they liked.

Do you remember how, in Dutee Chand's case, the Court of Arbitration for Sport said the IAAF had failed to prove that women with naturally high levels of testosterone had a competitive edge? Well, the IOC statement urged the IAAF to go back to that court with arguments in favour of reinstating the rule. The IOC was not advocating for discrimination, certainly not. "To avoid discrimination," the statement read, "if not eligible for female competition, the athlete should be eligible to compete in male competition." Translation: "We know XY females are really guys, but we want the world to think we're being fair."

Culbert said to me, tongue in cheek, "Congratulations, Kristen. You've changed Olympic policy." Our fight had just escalated.

Amanda Worley is a discipline counsel at the Law Society of Upper Canada, which means she litigates against bad lawyers. February 29 was a Monday. On the Wednesday before, Amanda took me to court with her, so I could observe two cases. I was about to take on a powerful international opponent, and I'd never been to a courtroom in my life.

In those solemn surroundings, what I was about to undertake suddenly felt real, and overwhelming. It didn't help that every courtroom drama I'd ever seen was crashing around in my head.

On Friday, the day we would learn who our Superior Court justice would be, I was too nervous to sit still. I took Arya for two long walks. Late that night, Brenda phoned with the name: Harriet Sachs. This was terrific news. Sachs, wife of the litigator Clayton Ruby, is a champion of women's and human rights law. When it comes to diversity issues, she has wide knowledge and experience. We knew we'd have a fair shot.

Just after midnight on Sunday, Brenda phoned again. "The IOC doesn't want to appear tomorrow," she said. "They want you to sign a letter to release them. They want to move this to April." April was when the other three organizations were to appear at the tribunal.

I was furious. This Superior Court appearance had been their ploy. We'd spent time and resources preparing for it. Were they turning tail because they'd seen Justice Sachs's name? "I will not release them," I said. "I want them in court on Monday at 10 a.m., as they requested. I want the world to see they were here." Culbert agreed.

On Monday morning, Culbert and her boss, Toby Young, who was going to make the Superior Court argument, brought me in through a side door. I was too nervous to face the media. Many athletes had shown up to hear this; the Worleys and my friend Janice Forsythe were there for me. UCI had an assistant lawyer there to monitor the proceedings.

The IOC's counsel—a litigator, not a human rights lawyer—tried to hand the IOC's new, bogus policy to Justice Sachs. She replied, "Sir, that's inappropriate." I burst out laughing, and my lawyers shushed me. But I couldn't help it. For the first time, I realized that the IOC was more afraid of me than I was of them. Then the IOC lawyer . . . agreed that the tribunal had the jurisdiction to rule on the IOC's motion to dismiss. And that was that.

What a mind game. Make everyone show up for court, ready for a full hearing, and then change your mind. But I was glad. I wanted to see, in April, all the organizations together in one room. I wanted them to see me.

The stage was set. The showdown was about to begin.

CHAPTER NINE

The Hearings

《 《 《 • 》 》 》

The Human Rights Tribunal of Ontario sits in a huge hearing room in a secure office tower at Bay and Queen Streets in Toronto. On one side of the room, a wall of windows faces west over Bay Street, nineteen floors below.

As in most courtrooms, the justices sit behind an elevated bench. On this day in April 2016, five rectangular oak tables were arrayed in a row below the bench. Because my table, on the far right of the room, was fully occupied by my legal team, I had to sit at the end, with my back to the Bay Street windows. The justice was to my right, the court spectators to my left. Which meant that I was looking down the length of all five tables: My team, headed by Brenda Culbert. The two lawyers for Cycling Ontario.

Two for Cycling Canada. Two for UCI. Two for WADA. The IOC didn't have a table—they were waiting for the tribunal to agree that it had no jurisdiction over them, so they just had a guy in the back taking notes. They were ostentatious in their absence.

Our adjudicator, Jo-Anne Pickel, had been on the tribunal since 2000. She is also a professor of law and a partner in a law firm, where she focuses on written advocacy, administrative law, constitutional law, labour and employment law, and human rights. She co-authored a paper, "Enforcing Human Rights in Ontario." All of that made me optimistic that she'd give my arguments a fair hearing.

I was strangely calm. Whatever happened now, I had done this. I had brought the plight of diverse athletes to the attention of these major organizations. I had made them take it seriously. I had made them assemble here to address it. The most powerful organizations in sport were here, on Canadian soil, because of something I started.

My friend Janice Forsythe had come into town for this, as she had for the (aborted) Superior Court proceeding. The night before, she'd taken me out to dinner. Afterward, we went back to where she was staying and contacted supporters for a few pep talks. We Skyped Renee Anne Shirley, the former head of Jamaica's anti-doping agency. (She and I had supported each other via email over the years.) Then we Skyped my friend Mianne, who was rollerblading in Adelaide.

After a restless night, I got up at six to take Arya for a walk in the park. At seven, I flipped on CBC TV's national morning news, so the sound would keep Arya company while I was gone. The lead story: Prince had died. The second story: the scandal-plagued Canadian senator Mike Duffy had been indicted for fraud. The third story was . . . me. The last image I saw as I walked out the door was a picture of myself, as Heather Hiscox talked about my case.

I thought I would charge my phone as I drove downtown, but it kept ringing—friends and reporters asking me if this was really happening. All I could manage was a dry, "Rumour has it." I picked up Janice near Queen and Carlaw. We parked in the underground garage and stepped into the elevator. Three teams of lawyers got on with us. I knew who they were: counsel for CC, UCI, and WADA, all looking grave. They knew who I was, too, of course. I said, "Good morning, gentlemen," and then pretended I didn't notice they were staring at me.

The gallery in the hearing room was two-thirds full. The Worleys were there, along with some of my athlete friends. I spied Greg Mathieu, CEO of Cycling Canada. I also saw a mysterious man I'd noticed before, in Superior Court. I was convinced he was with the Canadian government. This case held a risk for them: if a human rights violation was proved, under the Canadian Charter, Canada would be bound to pull out of UCI and the IOC until the problem was fixed. No Canadian cyclists in any international races. No Canadian athletes in the Olympics.

That was a big worry for me. I was fighting so that more athletes could be included in sport. If the case went the wrong way, all of Canada's athletes would be excluded. I would be the most loathed person in sport.

This first hearing was a motion to dismiss, so no evidence was presented. We couldn't submit doctors' reports, genetic papers, witness statements, or anything like that. At this point, all Culbert was trying to prove was that the tribunal did have jurisdiction in these matters. Essentially, our argument was, "All these bodies are connected, Tribunal. You have to look at where the control is. It starts with the IOC. They have a constitution that states, in so many words, 'If you want to participate in the Olympics, you must follow our rules.' The rules about allowable drugs are set by WADA. The UCI follows those rules, and so on down the line. You may not see that yet, because you haven't seen the evidence. But please don't dismiss this motion, because we want to show you how this game is run. Once we do that, you'll see that it's the international players who run it—affecting our lives here in this province."

Under the Ontario human rights code, a complaint has to fit into one of three "social areas": housing, employment, or services. Culbert argued that my cycling licence was a service agreement, and that agreement bound me to all the organizations. She argued that the connection was obvious: I couldn't compete unless I signed my licence with OCA. OCA followed the rules set by CC, and so on up the chain. Therefore, there was an implied service relationship among all these sports bodies. You couldn't artificially distinguish between WADA and the others, because WADA set the rules and the others had no choice but to follow them.

We were pretty confident about that argument when it came to the Ontario Cycling Association and Cycling Canada. They don't make up their own rules about TUEs or anti-doping regulations. They, along with the 185 other countries that follow the UCI licence system, copy, cut, paste and apply the rules they're given. But if those rules were in violation of the Canadian Charter, the Canadian bodies should fix them, not follow them.

We were less confident about the three international organizations. They all had various arguments as to why the tribunal, as a provincial human rights body, did not have jurisdiction over them. The IOC's argument, which they'd filed, was that my action was "out of time." That is, too much time had gone by between 2005, when I first signed my race licence, and 2015, when I filed my application to the HRTO. (Under Ontario's human rights code, a person usually has only one year from the date of the discriminatory action to file a complaint.)

I'd asked Culbert, "Can't we make the argument that I had no choice in 2005, and only now did I realize I could bring this action?" She explained that yes, a person can make that argument if she has a reasonable explanation as to why she's out of time. But it's a difficult case to prove, a high threshold to meet. She felt the tribunal would probably decide that, since I had the capacity and ability to bring this application earlier, there wasn't a legitimate reason that I hadn't.

At the hearing, the lawyer for UCI went first. He claimed that UCI was not in a service relationship with me—they set the TUE and gender-testing rules, yes, but setting rules isn't the same as providing a service. He also gave a long speech defending those rules: "Testosterone is an anabolic steroid, and those who take it have a competitive advantage." (Not true.) "Kristen is asking for exceptions to our rules." (Again, not true—I was challenging their basis.) There was no mention of my human rights concerns about gender verification and the discrimination against XY females.

WADA went last, and its lawyer spoke for eighty minutes. He, too, delivered a public service announcement about drugs, which ran like this: "We are the global authority on anti-doping, the overseer of sport. We hold all legal rights and controls." To me, he seemed to be trying to intimidate the justice by impressing upon her how powerful WADA is. Finally he got around to making the same argument as UCI had: that WADA's anti-doping regulations did not constitute a service agreement.

Throughout, his tactic was to repeat himself, becoming louder and more insistent as he went. As I watched, I realized who he reminded me of: Jim Jackson. To me, it seemed as if the WADA lawyer wanted the world to see his organization as noble, but was willing to bully anyone who didn't. When people like that feel threatened, their hackles rise. "How dare you question my authority?" they thunder. But I was through with being bullied.

Finally, Justice Pickel spoke. "This is unprecedented," she said. "None of us has been here before." She promised a decision in three months. You could see everyone in the room counting, "May, June, July." With the Rio Olympics looming on August 5.

Janice, the Worleys and I went back to Leslieville and had a beer. For the next three months, I tried to return to my normal life, to catch up on everything I'd let slide. People were emailing and calling me about the case, but I focused on my job and my private life. I'd taught myself to turn my passion for this issue on and off, or else it owned me. Still, the hum of worry—what if this was all for nothing?—was always in my brain, like a radio at low volume.

On July 20, 2016, Justice Pickel gave her decision. It was a mixed bag. First, her terminology wasn't ideal. She wrote that I "identify as an XY transgendered athlete." Not true. I don't "identify as" that. I am that, an XY female. Her suggesting otherwise demonstrates that even well-meaning people have more to learn, and highlights the vulnerabilities in the legal system.

Second, she dismissed my application against the IOC as out of time, and she dismissed my application against WADA because it wasn't a service agreement. We'd expected the finding about the IOC, but the one about WADA was a blow. We really felt we'd shown sufficient reason to push them forward to a full hearing. (Later, we filed a reconsideration request—basically, "Can you rethink this?"—but Justice Pickel denied it in September 2016.)

Still, there was good news: the tribunal accepted that it had jurisdiction over OCA, CC—and UCI. An international body based in Switzerland had to answer to Ontario human rights law. That was a big victory for the Human Rights Legal Support Centre, and for me.

We now faced a choice: Did we go straight into a merits hearing, present my evidence, trot in a host of medical experts? Or did we try mediation first?

Culbert almost always recommends mediation. She explained to me that the outcome of litigation is unknowable. There are many moving parts. You don't know how witnesses will perform, or what documents will be disclosed. At the end of the day, you might end up with nothing. With mediation, on the other hand, there's no downside. You just meet and talk, to see whether there's an appetite to settle. You don't have to agree to anything, and you can always move on to litigation afterward.

While the idea of presenting my case was exciting to me, the idea of mediation was even more exciting. What if, instead of fighting and trying to tear each other down, we had everyone in a room working together on the issues? Maybe we could actually resolve them. The other parties agreed, with the understanding that if a settlement couldn't be reached, we'd go to trial.

I felt a deep satisfaction. I'd done my best. I hadn't hit a home run, but I'd gotten on base. I showed that Canada's human rights laws could reach into an international sport organization. I'd opened the door—the floodgates!—for other athletes in other countries to bring human rights complaints of their own. Now dozens of sluggers like me can line up to bat. I know that one day soon we'll all come home for the win.

In May 2017, I entered mediation with the Ontario Cycling Association, Cycling Canada, and the Union Cycliste Internationale. The night before, Amanda's son Hartley, who was fourteen, called me. "Are you afraid?" he asked.

Hartley plays hockey. "When the Zamboni goes off the ice, and you're ready to skate on?" I said. "That's how I'm feeling right now." I wasn't afraid. But I was keenly aware of how important this would be. I wanted to get it right for athletes globally.

That morning I woke up even earlier than usual, at 4 a.m. I took Arya for a walk and watched the sun come up in the park. Then I dropped the dog at Ali's for the day and went home to change into my court clothes. Ali and Amanda had advised me to wear a dress. I had all my choices, including some I'd borrowed from Ali, hanging around my room. But after I showered, I looked at them hanging there like bats, and thought, No.

I pulled on black-and-white checked pants and my favourite long black T-shirt. I put on a Gucci belt and a black jacket. I rolled up the sleeves and added some bracelets—my usual creative hardware. I put my hair up. I wanted to look professional, but not like someone else's idea of that. It was important that I felt like me.

I left my house at 8:10 a.m. The mediation was scheduled for 9:15. I took the subway, which I don't often do. Standing at the platform at Bloor and Yonge, waiting to change lines, I felt the hustle-bustle of the city, and thought, None of these people knows what I'm about to do. But in some way or other it will impact all of them. What a feeling.

The mediation was private. No friends could come, no supporters. Only Brenda and me. As I exited the subway turnstyle at Dundas, I felt the same surge of competitive energy that I felt before a bike race. But as I entered the building at Bay and Elm, I was at peace. This wasn't about me winning at litigation. I was there for the bigger play, trying to make it better for all athletes.

I gave my name to security, who sent me to the four-
teenth floor, a long hallway of rooms. Mine, room 17, was
identical to the others: fluorescent lights, beige industrial
carpeting, grey walls, Ikea conference table, four office
chairs on casters, and an easel with paper. It was 8:45. For
the next twenty minutes, I sat alone contemplating the
anonymous city view out my window.

I had a lot to think about. For so long, I'd been trying to
get the attention of my sport bodies, to address the problems of how they treat diverse athletes. I hadn't wanted to
sue them, but it proved to be an effective way to bring
them to the table. Justice Pickel had recognized that the
OCA, CC and UCI might have perpetrated a system that
caused harm. If today went well, no other athletes would
suffer what I had suffered. This was my chance to say,
with the help of a skilled mediator, "Here's what I think
the issues are: athlete wellness, inclusion, global opportunity, and policy based on science. Here's what I want you
to do: Stop sensationalizing, stop *other*-izing bodies like
mine and Caster's. Stop perpetuating the myths, and the
marginalization they cause. And here are some things
we might do to make this a more complete and progres-
sive system." As a friend of mine put it, I was there to take
the stupid out of the conversation.

HRTO mediations are usually half a day. Mine was
scheduled for a full day, because there were four separate
parties, and the issues were complex: Is anyone liable?

Will the remedy be compensatory (monetary), a public interest remedy, or both? What would a public interest remedy look like—rule changes at the organizations? Policy development? Education? Just for context, let's say an employer doesn't have a human rights policy. The HRTO could order the employer to create one, and/or train their employees in human rights laws and practices. The idea is that you want to promote understanding and compliance with human rights laws going forward.

Brenda arrived at 9:10, and then there was a knock on door. Mimi Jones, the lawyer for UCI, came in. She was a flamboyant type, big red scarf, glasses, blonde hair, big talker. She shook my hand and exited.

A minute later, another knock: Greg Mathieu from Cycling Canada, with his lawyers. They looked a bit humbled. As I said, if this mediation went wrong, it could lead to further hearings whose outcomes might shut down the sport of cycling in Canada. The shiny new $550 million Velodrome, which had been built for Toronto's Pan Am Games in 2015, would go unused. Ontario could no longer license agreements for World Cup cycling events. Canadian cyclists would not be able to participate in qualifying races, which means they couldn't race internationally or in the Olympics. If Canada were to host an Olympics, they would have to do it without any cycling events. Cycling is one of the biggest Olympic sports, and it's one of Canada's biggest sports in the summer games. Shutting all that down would ripple out to bike stores, manufacturers. It would destroy the race community.

HRTO justices hear cases, and they also do mediations. At 9:30 our mediator, Sheri Price, entered our room and introduced herself. She'd been a vice-chair of the tribunal, and had spent a dozen years practising labour and employment law on behalf of trade unions and employees before that. She'd presided over one of the more public cases in the tribunal's history—her ruling changed the gender qualifications on Ontario's drivers' licences—so she was familiar with some of the ideas I'd be putting forward. A Newfoundlander by birth, Price was five foot two, spirited, big-hearted, energetic. A bundle of energy in a blue suit. She'd recently had twins. The things she said suggested that she'd read a lot about me. My tension melted away.

Price laid out the day. OCA, CC and UCI were stationed along the hallway, each in a room of their own. Price would spend the first part of the day hearing each group's argument. Then she'd relay that information from group to group, and begin to seek solutions and compromises. I was braced for the worst. How could we fix this much history in a day? We might fight hard for an agreement, yet still end up in litigation. I was ready for that, but I didn't want it. Litigation is fractious, combative. I might lose. If I won, I might serve only myself. But I wanted to make positive change that would have lasting impact.

Culbert and I had two hours with Price. One hundred and twenty minutes to outline it all—my history, genetics and endocrine science, the misinformation upon which sport regulations were based. I knew my opponents would try to make this about me—Kristen didn't like her TUE. So I zeroed in on the science. I wanted the facts to demonstrate how my human rights had been violated. Price asked questions. In what ways had I been oppressed? How had they responded to me at different points along the way? She seemed to understand how big the scope of this was.

When I finished, Price asked me the same question Hartley had: "Aren't you afraid?" I told her I used to be. I used to wake up panicked for my life. But I've stopped thinking of the IOC and UCI as powerful international organizations. Once I got behind the intimidating brands, I saw the individuals for who they were: people stuck in the past, who refused to educate themselves because they were loath to lose any bit of their power. But they were dinosaurs, and if they kept clinging to all that, they were doomed to extinction.

Price moved on to the other organizations. She heard their cases, and presented mine. She was striving for a deal that would satisfy us all. She also had to show them what litigation would look like—to outline for them what was at stake if they were unsuccessful.

She was gone for two and a half hours. I sat with

Brenda for some of it, then went down to Bay Street to a sidewalk café. I had a coffee and a raisin cookie and watched the world go by. I texted with Ali and a few others. Then I got a text from Brenda—time to come back upstairs.

Brenda had warned me not to expect too much. So it was a little strange when Price bounded into our room. "Kristen, I think I have good news for you," she said. She grabbed the pad and started writing, in green ink, describing what a partnership with me would look like. "Advocate to UCI and the Canadian Olympic Committee/IOC/WADA to develop scientifically based standards for XY female athletes," she wrote.

Then she flipped to a second page and began writing how I might also advise the OCA and CC. She was talking so quickly I couldn't keep up. It was now 2:30 p.m., and our day ended at five. I had two hours to find language that would acknowledge my past pain and rewrite the future. "What are they actually offering?" I asked Price.

Brenda—I'll never forget this—put her hands together in a prayer pose. "Kristen," she said, "they're admitting that you're right. They're saying, 'Work with us.'" They had violated my rights, physiologically and emotionally. They had taken away my career and my health. They had adversely affected my livelihood and my relationships inside and outside sport. And now I was supposed to help them? I was shaken. When a battle you've been fighting for so long abruptly ends, you don't have a response to it. It doesn't sink in.

But the clock was ticking. "Sheri," I said, "in Canada, we can write great papers and make great promises, but we don't always carry them out. I won't participate in a settlement without actions attached to it." Cycling Canada might say it wanted to work in partnership with me, but what did that really mean? And UCI still answered to the IOC—wouldn't their promises to me be in conflict with the IOC?

It was now 3:30. Brenda ran around the corner to her office to discuss the situation with her team. We all agreed. We couldn't rush this settlement. We had a public responsibility to do this right. Five p.m. was way too soon. We needed another day. Price headed back down the hall to talk to the others.

I went back to the café and downed another coffee. Until I stood up again, I didn't realize how much the last hour had taken out of me. I was wobbly-legged.

For such a long time, no one had listened to me. I'd organized conference calls, I'd written op-eds, I'd sent thousands of emails. I'd lost nights of sleep, I'd lost friends. Behind my back, people in authority had called me crazy; to my face, my sport organizations had implied that I was a cheater. My opponents never thought this day would come. They never thought I'd be able to challenge them legally. Now they claimed they would finally listen to me. Now they said they wanted me to help educate them.

I was happy. But I was also angry. Why couldn't they have heard me years ago, when I tried to share the scientific information? I was as right then as I was now. Why make me suffer for so long? Why did I have to lose my cycling career? And now, after years of dragging this out, they wanted to rush me. *No.* If today proved nothing else, it proved that it was their turn to listen to me.

Just before Culbert came back to get me, I thought of something John Dalla Costa once told me: when you're pushing a boulder up a mountain, the closer you get to the top, the more isolated you are.

Culbert, Price and I reconvened in room 17. The tribunal rarely grants a second day for a settlement, but this time they had. All parties agreed to meet again on July 4, until 10:30 p.m. if necessary. The groups also agreed to interact over the next four weeks, to put some ideas in place.

I told Price, "Please let them know that I'm pleased to see the direction they've taken." I walked out with my head high.

I met my old Lorne Park friend K.C. for a drink at a nearby pub. We didn't stop smiling for two hours. Later, MP Randall Garrison, who pushed so hard for Bill C-279, tweeted, "Looks like the universe still bends toward justice, even if ever so slowly and requiring some determined tugging."

In July, all the parties met again to hammer out the language of our settlement. It was a fifteen-hour dialogue, the longest Culbert had ever experienced. Here's the gist of it:

None of the organizations admitted to wrongdoing and I did not withdraw my allegations. We all agreed no further action would be taken against one another. However, UCI recognized that the IOC and WADA were the bodies responsible for their policies, and it agreed in good faith to advance the following three principles to them:

1. Guidelines related to XY female athletes should be based on objective scientific research, from sources outside the organization.

2. Both the IOC and WADA should ensure that therapeutic use exemptions (TUEs) are set by medical personnel with appropriate expertise.

3. Both organizations should ensure that the time frames for the review of any TUE application, as well as any testing required during the span of the TUE, should be consistent among athletes applying for testosterone. We agreed that UCI couldn't control the outcome of the IOC and WADA's policies, but UCI agreed to advocate for my ideas.

As well, UCI invited me to present, via Skype or FaceTime at their next scheduled Anti-Doping Commission, on key measures that should be taken to ensure respect for XY female athletes and to uphold their rights; and to make a further presentation at their next scheduled Cycling Anti-Doping Foundation training for doping control officers, to explain the particular challenges experienced by XY female athletes.

OCA and CC also recognized that WADA and the IOC were the bodies responsible for their policies. They put out a joint statement with me that began, "Increasingly, national and provincial sporting organizations in Canada encounter challenges related to XY female athletes participating in sport. On June 30, 2015, Kristen Worley, an XY female athlete, commenced an application in the Human Rights Tribunal of Ontario, which brought attention to challenges faced by XY female athletes participating in sport. Ms. Worley has been a leader in her efforts to raise awareness and education in human rights in Canadian and international sport."

Additionally, they agreed to advance the same three principles as UCI had—to WADA and the IOC, and also to the Canadian Centre for Ethics in Sport, the Canadian Olympic Committee, Sport Canada, the Commonwealth Games Federation and the Canadian Minister of Sport. As well, the OCA and CC agreed to encourage those last five organizations to advance the same principles to the IOC and WADA themselves—so my message will be heard and repeated by all of them. Not only did they agree to do that, their counsel had to provide confirmation to Culbert that they had done it.

Moreover, the OCA and CC agreed to encourage the other organizations to ask the IOC to review its transgender guidelines; and they agreed to try to provide scientific information that would inform said review.

The OCA and CC also agreed to undertake an awareness and education program for the cycling community, including coaches, officials and event organizers; and they asked me to be a panellist at their next congresses, to discuss diversity and inclusion.

The OCA agreed that its policies weren't compliant with the Ontario Human Rights Code. (That was a big admission.) To fix that, it agreed to review and revise its code of conduct and ethics to ensure that it complies with the Ontario Human Rights Code, particularly in the areas of gender identity and gender expression. And it agreed to review and revise its discipline and complaints procedure to reflect that complaints will be investigated, and investigated properly. It agreed to post its revised policies on its website, and to provide training for them—in coordination with CC—to its coaches, officials, staff, volunteers and event organizers.

The OCA and CC agreed to do all that by December 1, 2017. Did we get everything we wanted? No. We gave a little, they gave a little. But we kept inching forward. We made people talk about it. We chipped away at their biases, got them to think about their knee-jerk responses: Why do you think that a woman being healthy is a competitive advantage? What evidence do you have to support that?

It wasn't exactly the dramatic outcome I'd envisioned when I filed the application. It wasn't the wish list I had at the start. But good things are going to come from it.

I keep remembering the feeling I had at the end of the first mediation day. It had been a long eight hours, tense, exhausting and exhilarating. Culbert and I had walked out of the HRTO building together and paused on the sidewalk to say goodbye. "Have we pushed the boulder over the mountaintop?" I asked her.

"You did that a long time ago," she replied. "This is just the next step."

The sun was shining. The streets were alive with people heading home. They didn't know that we'd just helped to change the world. But we did.

CHAPTER TEN

The Future

《 《 《 • 》 》 》

The last time I saw Arlene—in September 2016—was also the first time I'd seen her in nineteen years. We met on my birthday, at a little waterside restaurant in Gravenhurst. She came out to greet me at 1 p.m., wobbling, and I was surprised by how frail she was. (Later, I found out she'd had a stroke and heart valve replacement surgery.) But her eyes were the same.

I hugged her, and my own eyes filled with tears. Her response was pure Arlene: she patted me and told me not to cry.

Arya was with me. She needed a walk, and I needed to expend some of my nervous energy, so the three of us strolled down to the water. I tossed a ball, Arya swam.

Then I put Arya back in the car, and Arlene and I took a table on the deck.

At first, our conversation was formal, polite. As she asked me basic questions, I realized that she didn't know where I lived; she didn't have my address or phone number. She asked me about my legal case, and I filled her in. Then things edged toward confrontational.

Arlene told me, "If I had known about your gender dysphoria, I don't know what I would have done." But she did know, on some level. And she did nothing. After my transition, she continued to do nothing. I thought, "Realizing that you've been ignorant about something is not supposed to be the end of the story. It's supposed to be the beginning of a new story." But I didn't say anything.

Then, toward the end of lunch, she called my leaving the Jackson family "my choice." This time I did speak up, a little. I said that wasn't true—I had to leave to protect myself "from him." She asked, "Who?" I said, "You know who. You made the choice. You chose him." But she cut me off. "I'm having such a nice time," she said. "Let's not ruin it. Let's schedule another time in the future to talk about this."

She was eighty-one. She was broken, physically. I knew that an open confrontation would crush her. A few years ago I might have done it. But today, spelling everything out about Jim, forcing Arlene to hear me, would take me backwards, into a space that was painful to me, a space

I'd fought hard to get out of. She'd shown me that she didn't have the capacity to have a relationship with me—not even as a friend, let alone a mother. Why put us both through pain for nothing?

At 2:45, I caught her checking her watch. Instantly I knew: She had to get back to Jim. She hadn't told him she was coming. She'd carved out this two-hour window, in which she'd try her best to open her mind to me. But I knew when our time was up that she would close it again.

As I drove home, I was amazed how little it mattered. Arlene isn't a bad person. Just a limited one. She's been that way my whole life.

Nearly a year later, after my settlement hearing in July 2017, Arlene sent me an email. Someone had filled her in on the Ontario Human Rights Tribunal's decision. "I now understand more of what you've been through," Arlene wrote. I showed it to a friend; she handed my phone back to me, saying, "That could have come from anyone."

If Jim dies first, Arlene and I may grow closer. But I'm not waiting around for that to happen. Do I want to keep the door open? I don't know. It's taken me twenty years to get to this point, where I'm not constantly second-guessing my decision to distance myself from the Jacksons. I'm no longer afraid that society will shun me for abandoning my family, and assume it's my fault. I know what happened.

Interestingly, for the first time, instead of her customary "Arlene," Arlene signed that last email to me, "Mum."

She hasn't been Mum to me for decades. Maybe she's changing as well. Maybe, as long as we're alive, it's never too late.

Since my mediation, I've been busy. In September 2017, I flew to Brisbane to meet with six members of the organizing committees of the XXI Commonwealth Games. For six hours—the meeting segued into dinner—we discussed their policies around diversity and doping, and I filled them in on my experiences. One month later, in October, the Commonwealth Games Federation adopted its first-ever human rights policy statement. David Grevemberg, the chief executive of the federation, said that the statement "represents the next step in the CGF's commitment to embed human rights within our governance, management systems, development, events, fundraising and marketing." He also said that inclusivity and peace were at the forefront of the federation's concerns.

Six months after that, when the Games were held on the Gold Coast, Queensland, Australia, from April 4 to 15, 2018, it was the first major multi-sport event to achieve gender equality by hosting an equal number of events for male and female athletes. As well, its forty-four hundred participating athletes included three hundred para-athletes, competing as equals. I hope I played a small part in those advancements.

In November 2017, I flew to London to meet Andy Brown (Graham was much on my mind as I landed). We'd been invited to speak at the Play the Game summit, and had decided it would be fun to arrive by bicycle. Play the Game, which is held every two years, is the world's largest sport conference. Academics, journalists, officials and others come together to discuss sport at the local, national and international levels. The conference that year was in Eindhoven, the Netherlands, from November 26 to 30. Andy and I took a night ferry to Rotterdam, then rode the 140 kilometres up to Eindhoven, on bike paths almost the whole way.

A crowd of about two hundred filled the hall when Andy and I spoke. For two and a half hours, I outlined my case and its outcome.

Afterward, Brian Cookson, a past CEO of Union Cycliste Internationale, came up to me. He said, "I'm glad the mediation is over. I want you to know, it was all about the IOC." I just rolled my eyes at him, but it felt like a kick in the gut. We'd claimed in my case that there is a direct link between the IOC's policies and UCI's—if Cookson agreed, why didn't he stand up for me? Why did his former organization fight me?

After the conference, I travelled to Amsterdam to meet Dick Swaab, whose research had taught me so much. It was the first time we'd met face to face. He's in his mid-seventies now, but he was wearing a snappy blazer and running up and down stairs. "Nature is always evolving," he said to me. "It's society that doesn't like to change."

Then, on November 30, I went to Geneva to speak at the second annual Sporting Chance Forum, where 175 attendees discussed the human rights risks associated with mega-sporting events. As I outlined my case yet again, Thomas Bach, the president of the International Olympic Committee, was seated three rows in, directly in my line of vision. I asked, "How many women in this room have been gender tested?" I thought there would be three or four. Ten women put their hands up. We were from Canada, the US, Australia, Western Europe. Too many. A sisterhood to which no one wants to belong.

But I didn't despair, because I know that we're part of a global shift. The ideas that I believed in alone for so long, others are beginning to see, too. The change is happening. The key takeaway of the Sporting Chance Forum—that the rights and well-being of people must be the central focus of sport—is spreading through the sport world, and from there, to the world at large. Sport was my safe place, then my place to hide, then my enemy. Now it's my venue to bring about social change.

Here's proof that people can change: Just before the Rio Olympics in 2016, Hein Verbruggen sent me an email. Hein was president of UCI from 1991 until 2005; he was also a member of the IOC, and the chairman of the coordination commission for the Beijing games in

'08. "I was one of those grey-haired guys," he admitted to me. "As a caretaker of sport, I had a responsibility to get it right, and I did you wrong." He added, "What you've achieved is greater than any professional cycling career. The change that will come will benefit the world. You know more than we did, and we need your help to help us get there."

In January 2017, Hein sent me another email, a long one. It's so important to me, I'm including parts of it here. The brackets are mine, but the rest is all Hein:

You are unfortunately fighting in a world [of sport] where decisions are mostly political. The IOC will always try to have decisions [made] by their "own" people, whether their "own" people are experts or not. . . .

This is the issue with Arne [Ljungqvist]. He has been for 20 years the medical guru of the IOC, so he was involved in ALL medical issues, obviously also in those that were not his specialty. Whether it was anti-doping, the list of forbidden products, hematology or the transgender issue, it was Arne that had to decide. I do not exclude that he consulted other specialist/doctors but he took the final decisions and who could argue with him? He was the medical professor!! . . .

Then the second painful problem for you is the fact that these guys will NEVER admit to having made mistakes. And I have already explained to you that there is a total lack of control on the doings of international sports organizations so corrections are difficult, say virtually impossible.

So Kristen, I know very well what you went through and still are going through . . . praise for your fighting spirit for a just cause.

Take care,

Hein

PS: I will go into the hospital on Jan. 30 for a bone marrow transplant around Feb. 8.

Hein died on June 14, 2017. He didn't live to see my mediation results, but he came to see the truth—proof that, if you give people the right information, they can change.

But as Brenda keeps reminding me, there's a difference between the law and justice. The former doesn't always lead to the latter. So I've been exploring a civil suit against the IOC and WADA. I believe they should compensate me for the stress they subjected me to, and for the loss of my career. I also have a larger goal in mind. I'd like to begin and run my own non-profit, the Human Diversity in Sport Foundation. I want the IOC, and all sport organizations, to acknowledge that they discriminate against diverse athletes, and I want them to stop discriminating.

I dream of changing the way sport (and society) looks at gender. Sport organizations have spent decades requiring athletes to change their bodies based on a strict, binary social construct: "A person is either male or female, and each one of those looks a certain way and does not differ." My fervent hope is that people will come to accept the full spectrum of gender—and accept that gender issues are human rights issues. Maybe then, we'll be kinder to and more accepting of one another as human beings.

Sport is international. It's a vehicle through which we meet and understand one another. Canada has a chance to be a model for the world. The fact that I might have a part in that—perhaps, in some way, that's what I became Kristen to do.

I lost my first career, sport, to have this career, advocacy. I lost that life, where I was a divisive figure, to have this life, where I hope to be a link between people. Ultimately, it was the right thing for me. If I had been a decorated athlete, it would have been about me. Now it's about everyone. I might have had medals. Now I can have a legacy.

On a personal level, I continue to open up. The relationships I've had are stronger, and I'm forming new ones. Until recently, I wasn't sure that could ever happen. I'm reconnecting with old friends. It's my turn to take care of Deirdre, who took such loving care of me.

I'm so thankful for the Worleys, and for all the angels I've met along the way—like Ron Scarpa, my waterski coach in Florida. He's a conservative Italian Catholic, but when I told him I'd transitioned, he said, "I always knew this about you. I was waiting for you to figure it out."

In my own way, I'm grateful for the Jacksons—they withheld their love, but that made me a fighter. And I'm so grateful for my birth mother, Tess, who came halfway around the world to have me, and who brought me to exactly the right place. Canada is one of five countries in the world that have human rights tribunals capable of challenging groups like UCI. If she'd brought me to the US, we wouldn't be here right now.

In August 2017, I flew to New Zealand. I'd booked the ticket months before my mediation in July; regardless of the outcome, I knew Tess was the person I'd want to see when it was over.

After my long battle, it was odd to no longer be in fight mode. Who am I, if not the embattled athlete? What do I do next? I thought understanding my history would be a good first step. As I rolled my suitcase out my front door, I marvelled at how easy it is to go to the other side of the world: GO train, UP train, plane. I flew into Auckland and took a puddle jumper to Christchurch. The customs agent asked, "Anything to declare?"

"I'm travelling to see my birth mom," I said. "I have some maple syrup and some Canada sweatshirts."

"I've been doing this for thirty years, but I've never

heard that story," the customs agent said. "Welcome home."

When I was young, Arlene told me my story as if it were a fairy tale. Now I was seeing the reality: This is where I began. Tess and I have a history, yet we don't. We're different, yet we're alike. I was so nervous, it felt almost like an emotional dysphoria.

Tess's daughter Melanie, who's a jewellery designer, picked me up. Our first stop was to a framer, where I had a photo of myself with Arya framed. Tess's seventy-sixth birthday would happen at the end of my visit. It was the first time I'd celebrate with her.

Mel and I took her dog to pick up her daughters from school: Bonnie was six, Cleo nine. My nieces. Blonde, curly hair. Bonnie, especially, looks like me.

I stayed with Melanie and her husband, Neil, a furniture builder, for four days. We went hiking in the mountains, rode a gondola up the coast, went crabbing. My relationship with Mel was surprisingly easy, much easier than it had been with Jonathan and Jennifer. I kept thinking, "We share DNA." I'd learned the hard way that you can't deny your DNA.

On day five, Tess arrived. She'd driven herself across the South Island a day early—she couldn't wait for me to come to her. She got lost coming into town, so Mel and I drove to where she was to guide her in. I got into her car, a standard-shift Peugeot hatchback, to ride with her. Tess is tiny, and she sits right up against the steering wheel. She was shifting like a truck driver. I realized this must be weird for her, too. When she and I left on our road trip Saturday morning, she popped the clutch and stalled. Mel posted a picture on Facebook with the caption, "There goes Thelma and Louise."

Our first stop was Timaru, about four hours down the coast. Tess's ancestors were Swedish immigrants who were among the first settlers. In the early 1910s, her paternal great-grandparents and their eleven children were such a presence that the road to their family farm was named for them, Lynch Road. Tess showed me the farm, where she was born and where her father was a sheep-shearer; she told me how she, her brother Jack and her sisters Kathy and Mary spent their lives outdoors. She showed me the family cemetery, where five generations of her family (my family!) are buried; where she went to school, where she rode her bike on the gravel roads. We saw a lot of sheep.

We had lunch near the canal, watching the ships. (Timaru is one of the southernmost ports in the world.) I thought about my birth father, Hugh, sailing in and out of that port.

Then we drove three hours to Dunedin, where Tess's younger sister Kathy lives with her husband, Terry. (Their daughter Theresa also flew in for my visit.) For the first few days, Tess kept suggesting things to do, to see. Gently,

I kept telling her, "All I want is time." I was happy if we just sat and had tea, and I could touch her arm.

Leafing through photo albums, I gradually heard the full story of how I came to be. Tess is short of stature but long on verve. The family photo album is full of shots of her posing in fancy dresses, or at dances with handsome men, skirts swirling. "You were busy," I said to her, which made her blush. I kept seeing my wavy hair, my chin and mouth, my pale-blue eyes, the colour of a glacier in the snow.

When Tess was twenty-four, Kathy took her to a party, where Terry introduced her to Hugh. They made a lively, logical foursome. Except for one fact: Hugh was married. He was handsome, though, with a pile of gorgeous hair. He seemed glamorous. After one night of dancing and drinking, they ended up back at Kathy's and Terry's home on Nelson Street, and Tess ended up pregnant.

Two months in, she boarded a ship for the six-week journey to Toronto, via Los Angeles, then through the Suez Canal and on to New York. A photo of her on board shows her lying on deck, on her stomach on an orange towel, wearing a red one-piece bathing suit, reading a book. From New York she made her way north, and arrived in Toronto in March 1966, visibly pregnant. She got a job as a nanny for a family in the tony neighbourhood of Forest Hill. Her employer, a businessman, would have a few drinks and bring home his partners to look her over. Why not? She was obviously a loose woman. Terrified, she'd lock herself into her basement bedroom. And then one day, walking down Spadina Road, she walked into David McKee's medical practice.

As we talked and laughed, I could see that for all of us, this visit was about healing. I'd been living in one kind of distress, and I saw that Tess had been living in another. She'd given me up, but she wanted to be in my life. She told me that if I hadn't found her by the time I turned fifty, she would have reached out to David McKee to find me. Even Terry's feelings were complicated: while we played golf one afternoon, he took pains to assure me that he would never have introduced Tess to Hugh if he didn't think he was a good guy.

"You were brave to come here," Terry said to me, more than once. That surprised me. I suppose if things had gone another way, I might have left with a broken heart. But to me, this visit didn't feel risky. It felt necessary.

From Dunedin, Tess and I drove eleven hours across the island, through lowlands and old mining towns, up narrow mountain roads with no guardrails. We arrived in Greymouth, where Tess lives now, in pitch dark and pouring rain. Tess's house is very English—coal heat, single-pane glass, chickens in the garden. I slept in Melanie's old room. The walls are lined with pictures of Tess's children and grandchildren. There was a space where she'd once hung a picture of Chris. I gave her the one I'd framed of me and Arya, and she put it up right away. "It fits perfectly," she said.

I spent time with Katrina; her husband, Richard; and their two children. For the first time, I met Tess's husband, Barrie, a lovely, gentle man in his eighties. He hadn't known a thing about me the night I first called Kathy, but he accepted me immediately. But mostly, I focused on Tess. I'd bring her coffee at 7 a.m., and we'd sit in our PJs and yak.

We talked about the struggle we had after our first meeting, how Tess would call me eight times a day. "We're going to do it differently this time," I promised her. "We know better now." Just before I left, Tess gave me an early birthday present, a necklace made by Melanie. On it is a disc, inscribed with "9/19/2017"— my birthday—and "Love, Mum." I never take it off.

As the plane lifted, I thought back to a conversation Tess and I had on the first day of our road trip. "Think about what we're doing right now," I'd said to her. "You dropped me off as a baby boy on the other side of the world. Now I'm a grown woman, driving your hatchback on this two-lane highway, touring your life. My whole life has been a search for my identity. Now I'm looking at it."

After all those years and all those miles, there we were, mother and daughter. It could hardly be more complicated. Yet it couldn't be simpler.

"Well, you know," Tess replied, "that's just the way life is."

When I got back home, I sent Tess an iPad, so we could Skype. These days, we chat three or four times a week. She'll call me when she's cooking dinner, or when I'm out walking Arya. It's lovely.

I no longer feel like I'm fighting. I don't wake up afraid anymore. I'm at peace. I've gone through another transition, and I like who I am: a boy who could never be what people wanted him to be, who fought back until I became the woman I always knew I was.

ACKNOWLEDGEMENTS

« « « • » » »

This book is dedicated to Graham Worley, who never wavered in the most difficult and challenging times as my stepfather. Graham taught me great lessons in life and in death about the human experience; about compassion, perseverance and commitment, and how to believe in one's self and not be afraid. Life is a journey, and it is what we do with the brief time we are here, and the positive impact we have, that matters. I hope to leave the world a better place than it was when I first arrived.

To Deirdre, Alison and Amanda, for your unconditional love and support. Like Graham, you never wavered in the most challenging times, continually teaching the importance and values of family and of being there for each other no matter the unique struggle one is going through.

To Janice Forsyth, Renee Anne Shirley, Andy Brown, Jeff Adams and Brendan Schwab. I am so blessed to enjoy your personal friendships, and I admire your continued commitment to creating awareness, educating, and implementing change in policy and society in general. Thank you for working to make the sporting system inclusive and universally accessible, and truly representative of those living in Canada and around the world.

To Brenda Culbert, Dr. Galea, Dr. Swaab and Dr. Noakes. I am so grateful to each of you for your compassion and your expertise in the law and sciences. You exemplify a personal and professional commitment to challenging the status quo and improving the lives of others. It is truly a calling to commit one's life to this work. Your deep knowledge was essential to our success, and has and will continue to put the wheels in motion within and outside of the international sports system.

There is a common theme among the people who have touched my life: these are people who never wavered when I needed them most, and at times received relentless pushback from the sports authorities who opposed my claims. These allies helped ground my work in strong principles, science and law, creating a fundamental knowledge base, which led us to this success.

The expression 'it takes a village to raise a child' resonates with me. This was truly the case; without help and encouragement, I would not have become the better person I am from this journey, and our successes would not have been possible. Thank you to Johanna Schneller for her eloquence in helping me to tell this story.

And lastly, to my mother Margaret (Lynch) Brown. This all began in a small farming town on the east coast of the South Island of New Zealand. None of this would have been possible without you making the decisions and sacrifices you needed to make half a century ago to ensure a better life for me. Your support has allowed me to pursue my dreams.

This has been an incredible journey and I feel so fortunate to be able to share this story. Some athletes were destined to compete and win medals for their nation. That was not my athletic journey—I was destined to take an entirely different direction to create awareness, educate and implement policy change on behalf of women athletes around the world.

I would not hesitate to do it all over again.

Thank you.

Kristen Worley

« « « « « • » » » » »

I'm so grateful to all of Kristen's friends and associates for giving me their time and their invaluable assistance, especially K.C. Bascomb, Andy Brown, Brenda Culbert, Janice Forsyth, Anthony Galea, Tim Noakes and Dick Swaab. A million thanks to the Worley family for opening their home and hearts, and to Amy Moore-Benson for introducing me to Kristen. And my everlasting thanks to Kristen: we cried, but we also laughed a lot.

Johanna Schneller

INDEX

« « « · » » »

Allen, Ardith, 99

androgen insensitivity syndrome, 92

Armstrong, Lance, 136–37

Arya (dog), 167, 178, 183, 190, 218

Ash, Mr., 40

AthletesCAN, 115, 116, 135

"Promising Practices," 138–39

Athletic Federation of India, 164

Athletics South Africa (ASA), 143

autogynephilia, 74

Bach, Thomas, 208

Bagger, Mianne, 130–31, 133–34, 182

Bailey, Donovan, 153

Bain, Jerald, 147

Bala Manor, Muskoka, 11–16, 24, 38–39, 59, 68–70

Bannister, Roger, 53

Bascomb, K.C., 197

Bassett, Carling, 33

Beach, the (Toronto), 49, 52–53

Bella (dog), 98, 149, 167

Bhanot, Lalit, 136

Bill C-279, 156–58, 197

Birch-Jones, Jennifer, 116

Blanchard, Ray, 73–74, 75

Boileau, Martin, 158–59

Bolt, Usain, 142

brain-sex science, 89–92

Braniff, Heather and Dan, 30

Brassard, Pierre, 100, 105

Brown, Andy, 142–43, 159, 163, 207

Brown, Anne, 149–50

Brown, Barrie Ernest, 6, 217

Brown, Bonnie, 213

Brown, Cleo, 213

Brown, Katrina, 6, 56, 60, 62, 217

Brown, Melanie, 6, 56, 60, 213–14, 216, 217

Brown, Neil, 213

Bush, Jim, 29, 30

Canadian Association for the Advancement of Women in Sport (CAAWS), 115, 116, 136

223

KRISTEN WORLEY is a former world-class cyclist and now an international inclusivity and diversity advisor, educator and public speaker. She is the first athlete to legally challenge the gender policies of the International Olympic Committee and related international sports bodies, which she successfully argued were designed to discriminate against female athletes. She lives in Toronto.

« « « « · » » » » »

JOHANNA SCHNELLER is one of North America's leading freelance journalists specializing in entertainment features. Her weekly Fame Game column in the *Globe and Mail* has been nominated for four National Newspaper Awards. She lives in Toronto.